Fire It Up and Floor It
Ingram Spark

Shift Out of Neutral Into a Faith That
Goes Somewhere
Greg Smith

GospelChariot LLC

GospelChariot LLC

Reach me online: www.gospelchariot.com

ISBN Digital Online: 979-8-9991032-0-8

ISBN Paperback: 979-8-9991032-1-5

Contents

Introduction

M ost people aren't lacking for knowledge. They're aching for movement. They need ignition.

They've listened to the sermons. They've read the books. They've underlined the right verses and nodded along with the podcasts. But the engine is still cold. The wheels haven't turned. They're still parked in the driveway. Something's stalled. And beneath the surface, a deeper question lingers:

How do I move from knowing about faith... to actually living it?

This book is for those who are tired of drifting, frustrated with circling the block spiritually, and outdone with pretending everything is fine while the soul stays stuck in neutral. You're not asking for noise. You're longing for traction. You want a faith that actually pulls you forward.

You're not alone. Countless others have stood where you stand—longing for clarity, craving direction, and aching for a faith that moves.

Fire It Up and Floor It is not a guide to spiritual maintenance. It's a call to ignition. It's the first step in a journey that refuses to settle for shallow sentiment. It presses into surrendered obedience.

The road is already paved. The pavement isn't your effort or worthiness. The pavement is Jesus—through grace, by faith, with power. The path is not a theory. It is a Person. He does not wait at the finish line. He walks beside you. And He knows the way.

That road has a name. Isaiah 35:8 describes it like this:

And a highway will be there; it will be called the Way of Holiness.

That's the road we're traveling. And this book is only the beginning.

This book launches the *Highway to Holiness* series—a journey designed to help you shift from passive belief to active, obedient, purpose-filled life in Christ.

Here's the road ahead:

- **Fire It Up and Floor It** – Starting the journey with Jesus

- **The Holy Spirit: Fueled by Fire** – Learning to live by His power, not your own

- **Looking Through the Windshield** – How faith in Jesus changes the way you view the world

- **Looking in the Rearview Mirror** – Navigating past mistakes and learning to forgive yourself

- **Dodging the Potholes** – How Satan attempts to wreck faith

- **When the Rubber Meets the Road** – Putting it all together in a powerful, passionate life

- **The Final Destination** – Keeping eternity in view

You're not just holding a book. You're stepping into a journey. One that doesn't merely inform your mind, but reshapes your walk. One that moves you from sitting still . . . to stepping forward. From "almost there" to "let's go."

In this first volume, you'll discover what it truly means to start. You'll discover the central figure—Jesus Christ—and what He accomplished. You'll explore how grace lays the foundation, how faith takes the wheel, how confession anchors your identity, how repentance transforms your path, how baptism unites you with Christ, and how piety sustains your forward motion.

But none of this is meant to stay on the page. Each chapter invites you to surrender more fully, to walk more boldly, and to trust the One who has already paved the road ahead. So here's your moment. Not to figure everything out or wait until the timing feels right, but to trust the One who calls you forward and has already paved the way ahead.

The key is in the ignition. The engine is ready. Now is the time to move.

There are a few personal convictions I hold in how I write, especially when speaking of God. I choose to capitalize every pronoun that refers to God—not because grammar demands it, but because reverence does. I also italicize Scripture, not for emphasis alone, but to set apart the voice of God from every other word on the page. You may notice these choices throughout my writing. They are not conventions. They are confessions. And I offer them with the prayer that they honor Him more than they distract you.

Leaving the Driveway

Saying Yes to the Journey, Even If You Don't Know the Route

G od did not intend the road to salvation to be difficult, complicated, or obscure. By the road to salvation, I mean the "how-to." Think in terms of a map. How do I get from point A to point B? How do I journey from lost to saved? From sinner to saint? From eternally damned to eternally blessed? How do I inherit eternal life? That is what this book is about.

At one time, DiAnne and I rented a convertible each year for a weekend trip. Oddly enough, after we bought a convertible, we quit taking the trip. The rules were playful but strict: the driver couldn't look at the map or question the navigator. Only four directions were allowed—left, right, straight, or turn around. No four-lane highways unless absolutely necessary. No hotel reservations. And we had to play a round of golf along the way.

The objective was simple. Spend time together without plans, and embrace whatever came our way. We meandered down country roads, pausing at sights that we (mostly me) wouldn't normally stop. I didn't mind browsing in an old country store or antique store. After all, I had nowhere in particular to go. Not having a destination was my biggest struggle. I was patiently impatient.

Very rarely do I look at a physical map anymore. I usually get turn-by-turn directions from a GPS-enabled smartphone or my fancy Apple Watch. It just vibrates when I need to turn. "Turn left in ½ mile." "Turn right in 500 feet." "You have arrived at your destination." "Your destination is on the right." You get the idea. The thoughts in this book aren't turn-by-turn directions. The actions aren't required to be done in a certain order. In fact, they aren't designed to be orderly. As you will read, they are expressions of faith.

God Doesn't Play Hide-and-Seek

One Sunday afternoon, my fortune cookie read, "You are almost there." "Almost where?" I thought. I don't want to journey through life thinking I'm "almost" some place I didn't even know I was going! God does not intend for you to wander aimlessly searching for salvation. God doesn't intend for you to spend your life wondering if "you are almost there." God provides confident assurance of your eternal destination and clear direction.

For you are saved by grace, through faith, and this is not from you; it is the gift of God, not by works, so that no one might boast. (Ephesians 2:8-9)

Before we go too far, let's clarify something. Faith isn't the final objective. Relationship with God is the final objective. Heaven isn't the final objective. Relationship with God is the final objective. (I'm repeating that statement to make sure you understand how important it is.) Faith will become sight. Hope will become reality. Love will remain. Any attempt to find salvation without being primarily concerned about a relationship with God is doomed to failure. It is futile. Our intense yearning for a relationship with God is the fuel for salvation. We want to go to heaven because that is the place where God lives. We want faith because it is the path to a relationship with God. Every component of salvation begins and ends with God. God did not intend for the knowledge of salvation to be difficult. He isn't hiding Himself. He is making Himself known.

God wants you to find salvation. Did you get that? God wants to forgive your sin. God loves you. This book is a simple exercise in making sure you find salvation. Conversion is more than saying a phrase or raising a hand. Conversion is a deep commitment to become a follower of Jesus. It is rich in action and symbolism. It is an experience, not a moment.

It's easy to make a wrong turn. It's not difficult to take the wrong road. This book is about the right road. Most of us have been lost. Not just in a spiritual sense, but in a physical sense. Have you ever thought you knew where you were going when you got lost? Most of us don't start with the intention of getting lost. Maybe we don't want to stop and ask for directions. Maybe we ask for directions and become confused when we try to follow them. Maybe the person giving directions really didn't know what he was talking about. Maybe the GPS ran us in circles.

Several years ago, when DiAnne took the Architectural Exam, I went to Abrams Creek in Cade's Cove to fish for trout. DiAnne was taking exams all day, so I had free time. Fishing was a great way to pass the time. I hiked toward Abrams Falls, found a good place to get in the creek, and started fishing. I wasn't catching anything, but I was having a good time. It started raining, so I decided to get back on the trail and head to the truck. Out of the creek and up the hill I went . . . and went . . . and went, fighting through bushes and undergrowth, wondering what happened to the trail. When I got to the top of the hill, I knew I was in trouble. I should have crossed the trail. I stopped to listen. I could hear the creek on both sides of the hill! I was lost! I hiked back down to the creek and walked upstream. I knew I came from upstream, so I deduced it would eventually take me back to where I came from. At least close enough I would see someone. After an exhausting upstream hike through the water, I heard voices—a couple coming down the trail. I knew I was found. I was elated! I didn't intend to get lost. But I was happy I was found!

The Danger of Almost

We long for assurance. We need it like oxygen. We can't live in that dreadful space of "you are almost there" un-certainty. We will go out of our minds wandering aimlessly on a trip that goes nowhere. Almost saved. Almost faithful. Almost known by Jesus. Almost there, yet never arriving at a destination. Almost is a haunting word. Ask the five foolish virgins in Matthew 25. They carried lamps but no reserve of oil. They waited, but not with readiness. The door was shut, and they stood outside in the dark. Ask the rich young ruler, who held all the answers but walked away from the One who is the answer. Ask Judas, who kissed the Son of God and stepped into the night.

A road trip without a map, without signs, and without a destination is not a journey—it is a slow drift into despair. Yet many believers wander through life in just that way. They speak of hope, but their hope has no anchor. They speak of faith, but their faith has no foundation. They are sincere in their intentions, but sincerity is not the measure of salvation. If that were enough, the Pharisees would have stood justified.

The Pharisees were sincere. They practiced devotion with unmatched passion. They fasted with discipline. They tithed with precision. They prayed with eloquence and wore the Scriptures like badges of honor, binding them to their garments and flaunting their righteousness before men. They were respected. They were influential. They were religious to the core.

And still, Jesus looked at them and said, *Woe to you*. That should stop us in our tracks. If outward reverence without inward transformation earned a curse from the lips of Christ, then no amount of effort or fame can substitute for a heart aligned with God.

Jesus made statements that call for serious, deep self-evaluation. *Not everyone who says to me, "Lord, Lord," will enter the kingdom of heaven, but only he who does the will of my Father who is in heaven. Many will say to me on that day, "Lord, Lord, did we not prophesy in your name, and in your name drive out demons and perform many miracles?" Then I will tell them plainly, "I never knew you. Away from me, you evildoers."* (Matthew 7:21-23) Jesus is not vague. He doesn't leave room for misunderstanding.

Everything about the Pharisees looked devout. Their words were polished. Their behavior was measured. Their reverence was visible. They called Him Lord. They lived as though they were chosen. But Jesus uttered words that shattered every illusion: *I never knew you.* Let that sink in for a moment. Jesus didn't say, "I used to know you," or "You didn't do enough." He said, *I never knew you.* Those are not the words of someone disappointed. Those are not just words of failure. Those are words of final, permanent, terrifying rejection. Those are the words of a Judge rendering final judgment. And they should cause every heart to tremble.

We don't want to appear righteous. We want to be righteous. Since we tend to think the very best of ourselves, we need honest self-evaluation. We tend to grade ourselves on a curve. We give ourselves gold stars for good intentions, for trying hard, for doing better than we did last year. We assume God sees it the same way. We don't need assumptions; we need assurance. Wishful thinking and shallow comfort aren't enough. A misleading pat on the back won't suffice when the path is crumbling beneath our feet.

Jesus' words cut through the self-deception. He's not looking for performance. He's looking for relationship. Jesus demands obedience and surrender. We don't want to look righteous. We want to be righteous. We want to walk in the

Father's will — not our version of it, not a watered-down substitute, not a culturally acceptable remix.

And that means we have to get real. We must be brutally honest with ourselves. We must quit hiding behind good deeds. We must stop comparing ourselves with others. We must avoid resting in the applause of others or letting someone else determine our spiritual status. Brutal honesty demands we acknowledge our faults and failures.

This is not about checking spiritual boxes or keeping up appearances. It is about standing exposed before the King who searches every heart. He sees what is done in secret. He knows what is whispered in silence. And He doesn't ask for shallow gestures. When He says, *Follow me*, it is not a metaphor. It is a summons to surrender everything, to walk the path He walked, and to be truly known by the One who reigns. He isn't asking for attention. Jesus is asking for our lives.

So the question is simple. Do you know Him? And more importantly—does He know you? That's the only assurance that matters.

This book has one simple purpose: helping you find peace with God. It is for those who seek to know with **confidence** that God has saved them from sin. It is for those who want to make a serious commitment to God. It is not for the faint or the weak-hearted. It is for those with courage. This book isn't about "going to church" so you feel good about yourself. Discipleship demands total commitment. It proclaims dying to self. It demands living life as a new creation in Jesus Christ.

Anchored in Promises, Not Emotions

Your salvation isn't based on subjective feelings. Your salvation is based on objective promises from God. Your salvation isn't a mood. It isn't tied to how you feel when you wake up on a rainy Monday. It isn't stronger on the days you read your Bible and weaker on the days you don't. It doesn't rise and fall with your emotions.

Feelings are fragile. They shift with the wind. They're swayed by hormones, headlines, and heartbreak. You can feel lost when you're found. You can feel guilty even after you've been forgiven.

But your salvation is not built on your feelings. It's built on something far more solid. It rests on the character of God. It is confirmed by the cross of Christ. It is anchored on blood that speaks a better word than guilt ever could.

You're saved by grace through faith. That's not poetry. That's a promise. That's not a feeling you chase—it's a truth you stand on.

God doesn't save you because you feel sorry enough for Him to respond. He doesn't save you because your emotions finally match your doctrine. He saves you because you trust His Son. And when you put your faith in Jesus, He moves. Heaven moves. The Spirit seals. And your name is written.

This book is not written to make you feel better. It's written to make you *know* better.

That's why John wrote: *I write these things to you so that you may know you have eternal life—to those who believe in the name of the Son of God.* Your salvation isn't a guess. It isn't a gamble. You don't cross your fingers and hope. You know!

There's security in that knowing. There's peace in that promise. There's rest for the weary, wandering soul. So let's not confuse assurance with emotion. Let's not trade confidence for confusion. Let's anchor our faith, not in the waves of our experience, but in the bedrock of God's Word.

Let's start a journey. Let's ease off the brake and start down the road to peace and security. Let's dodge potholes, avoid wrong turns, and arrive safely in God's mercy.

The Road Ahead

But none of this matters—none of it—if we don't get Jesus right. You can memorize the map, repeat the directions, and mark every spiritual milestone, but if you misunderstand the One at the center of it all, you're still lost.

Salvation isn't a formula to memorize—it's a Person to follow. It doesn't begin with steps. It begins with Christ. He is not simply a good man or a wise teacher. He is not a metaphor or a moral example. He is the Son of God—the Lamb who takes away the sin of the world, the risen King who still calls, *Follow me.*

If we're going to fire it up and floor it, then we must know who is in the driver's seat.

In the next chapter, we ask the question that shapes everything: Who is Jesus? Not just in theory, but in your life. In your heart. In the road you're walking.

Because until you see Him clearly, the path will always stay dark. But once you do, every step begins to make sense.

Who Is Jesus?

When You Realize the Driver is the Destination

. . .unless you believe that I Am, you will die in your sins . . .

It's not uncommon to hear these words: "He/she was a good person." As if the path to heaven is being a good person. Heaven will be filled with bad people. You might react negatively when you read that. I mean, how could I say such a thing? Surely, I don't mean that heaven will be filled with murderers, adulterers, liars, cheaters, drug dealers, prostitutes, etc. I do. I mean that heaven will be filled with all those. Jesus said so. *I tell you the truth, the tax collectors and the prostitutes are entering the kingdom of God ahead of you.* (Mt 21:32) Jesus made that statement to people who considered themselves righteous. The point is simple and profound. Good people don't go to heaven. People who believe in Jesus go to heaven.

Simon, a Pharisee, invited Jesus to dinner. Most likely, it was the kind of meal where everyone knew their place. A woman walked in. It was common for an uninvited guest to join a meal, especially if a well-known teacher or rabbi was there. Hospitality was deeply rooted in Jewish culture. Someone of status, like Simon the Pharisee, might very well have a home with an open courtyard or semi-public area. This space would be great for entertaining guests. Others in town might stop and linger around the outer edges to listen in. The gatherings blurred the lines between public and private. The buzz of curiosity often drew a crowd.

A woman walked in. Her name isn't recorded in scripture, just her reputation. She was a woman from the streets. She was a woman who lived a sinful life. Her sinful life isn't specified. However, most suspect she was a prostitute. She entered Simon's house uninvited, unwelcome, and unashamed. It took great courage for the woman to approach Jesus in that setting. She wept at Jesus' feet. She wiped His feet with her hair. She poured perfume on His feet. Simon was critical, maybe even horrified. *If this man was a prophet He would know what kind of woman is touching Him, that she is a sinner.* (Luke 7:39)

Simon saw sin. Jesus saw love. Simon saw shame. Jesus saw acceptance. Simon saw rebellion. Jesus saw faith. Simon stayed immersed in sin. The woman walked away forgiven. The woman knew Jesus was the answer.

Who is Jesus? Jesus is the answer to humanity's problem.

The Problem Beneath Every Problem

If Jesus is the answer, what's the problem? Sin. Sin severs our relationship with God. The issue isn't that people mess up sometimes. The issue is sin. Not just mistakes. Not just flaws. Sin. The word feels heavy for a reason. It means something has gone terribly wrong. Sin breaks things. It breaks trust. It breaks people. But worst of all, it severs our relationship with God. Not because God is fragile, but because He is holy. His nature is pure. His justice is unflinching. He doesn't compromise truth to keep the peace. He doesn't pretend sin didn't happen. He can't ignore it. He won't. God's righteousness and holiness won't allow Him to turn a blind eye to sin.

Sin isn't a paper cut you slap a band-aid on. It's a mortal wound. It demands a cure deeper than good behavior or good intentions. Sin can't be overlooked. God will not wave a hand at sin as if it is unimportant. God hates sin because sin is the opposite of God's nature.

Sin falls into two broad categories: doing the wrong thing and not doing the right thing. For example, God forbids lying. So if one lies, he does the wrong thing. God instructs us to love our neighbor. If one fails to love his neighbor, he doesn't do the right thing. Here's the kicker. Everyone fails. Everyone sins. It's not just the rebels, the reckless, and the self-centered. Even those who are kind, loving, and careful commit sin. Everyone.

If you begin to name the struggles in your life, you will eventually discover that each one finds its origin in sin. Sin is the root beneath every sorrow, the thread that weaves through every wound. That may sound bold, even overstated—but it is true. Every heartache that lingers, every betrayal that cuts deep, every relationship that falls apart, every act of injustice, every addiction that tightens its grip, every war that rages, every lie spoken, every fear that paralyzes, every shame that haunts—when traced to their source, they all lead back to the same place. Sin is not just one of our problems. It is the problem behind them all.

It's not always your sin. Sometimes it's the sin of others. Sometimes it's the collective brokenness of a fallen world. But sin is always there, lurking as a crack in the foundation. Sometimes marriages fall apart because of selfishness, pride, or unfaithfulness. Those aren't surface-level problems. Those are sin problems. Sometimes people fall into financial ruin due to greediness or lack of self-control. Those are sin problems. Some people live in fear and guilt because of past mistakes or trauma. Those are the ripple effects of a world damaged by sin. We chase power, pleasure, and approval and find ourselves exhausted, anxious, and empty. That's spiritual misalignment with the way we were made to live.

Even physical suffering entered the world through the presence of sin. That does not mean that every illness is the direct result of a personal act of disobedience, as though all pain could be traced to a single misstep. But the existence of sickness, disease, and decay—the very shadow of death itself—is the consequence of sin's curse upon creation. In the beginning, there was no suffering, no groaning, no dying. God called His creation good, and there was harmony between heaven and earth, between body and spirit, between man and God. But when sin entered through Adam, death followed close behind. From that moment on, the human body became vulnerable to pain, brokenness, and mortality. As Paul writes in Romans 5:12, *Sin entered the world through one man, and death through sin, and in this way death came to all people, because all sinned.* This is the tragic inheritance of a fallen world—a world groaning under the weight of rebellion, where even our cells and bones bear the evidence of a broken covenant.

Sin is like rust. It eats away at what was once good. It corrupts what was made for beauty and wholeness. That's why you can't treat sin like a surface wound. It is a deep infection that requires a complete cleansing from within. You've got to dig deeper.

The Most Counterintuitive Insight

We are often convinced that our greatest problems live outside of us. We point to our circumstances, our enemies, our lack of time or money. We assume that if those things changed, peace would return. But Jesus flips that thinking on its head. He does not begin with what is around us. He begins with what is inside us.

The real issue is not the storm on the horizon. It's the condition of the heart. Sin takes root in our motives, in our desires, and in the places we refuse to surrender. And until the root is exposed, the fruit will remain rotten. You can try to fix the symptoms, but if you ignore the disease, the decay will continue. Trying harder may patch a few leaks, but if the boat is sinking, you need more than a patch. You need rescue.

If you take time to identify the struggles in your life and peel back each layer with honesty, you will eventually uncover sin at the center. Sometimes it's your own sin. Sometimes it's the sin of others. Sometimes it's the weight of a fallen world. But in every case, only Jesus has the power to redeem what sin has ruined.

We don't have the ability to fix it. We can't undo our sin. When it's done, it's done. We can't take it back. A thousand good actions won't negate a single bad one. It is not a credit/debit relationship. If we have more credits (good things) than debits (bad things), we are still condemned. It's not like banking. You can't pay off one sin by racking up a hundred acts of kindness. No amount of credits can negate one debit. Apologies won't remove it. Effort won't erase it. You can't give enough money that God will forget it. One sin poisons the well. One drop makes the whole glass undrinkable. Sin places us in the dark, damp cell of a hideous, horrible prison.

The Only Cure That Reaches the Root

There is only one solution to the problem of sin: Jesus Christ. The answer will never be found in self-improvement, in religious effort, or in measuring ourselves against others. No amount of personal effort can cleanse what has been corrupted. No moral achievement can erase the guilt that sin leaves behind. The gospel is not a path to becoming more respectable. It is the divine announcement that only Christ has the power to cure our sin problem.

Jesus didn't step into our world to treat symptoms. He didn't come to brush sin off like lint or give us coping mechanisms. Jesus came to rip sin out by the root. He came to destroy the curse that poisoned the earth. Jesus must go deeper than behavior to do that. Jesus transforms the heart: your heart. He came to remove the guilt that condemns us. He came to bear the wrath that justice demands. He came to restore the relationship that sin had shattered. The cross is not a religious emblem. The cross is a transaction.

God's justice demanded payment. A sinless man had to take our place. That man was Jesus. He carried the weight of the world's rebellion on His shoulders. He shed blood that wasn't stained by the guilt of sin. He died a death He didn't deserve to give life we couldn't earn. The story of Jesus isn't about being nice. Jesus' mission was a rescue mission. It was planned in eternity before creation was born.

That is why Jesus stands at the center of history, of Scripture, and of salvation itself. That's why faith in Him isn't optional. Jesus is not a side dish. He's not a religious flavor you add to your life.

Faith in Jesus is indispensable for salvation. Jesus came into this world to save sinners. Only Jesus can repair man's relationship with God. You need Jesus. There is no other path to salvation. He is the only one who can pay the debt for your sin. No other teacher, prophet, or philosopher can reach that deep or heal so completely.

Before you declare faith in Jesus, you've got to know who He is. Not simply by gathering facts or repeating familiar stories. Jesus is not a figure confined to history or a name printed on a page. You need to know the One who gave Himself for you and rose again so that you could be new.

I AM

And he said to them, "You are from below; I am from above. You are from this world. I am not from this world. Therefore, I said to you, 'You will die in your sins', for if you do not believe that I Am, you will die in your sins." And they said to him, "Who are you?" Jesus said to them, "Just what I have been telling you from the beginning. I have many things to say and to judge concerning you, but the one who sent me is true, and what I heard from him I declare to the world." They did not know that he was speaking to them about the Father. Therefore, Jesus said to them, "When you see the Son of Man lifted up, then you will know that I Am. I do nothing from myself, but just as the Father taught me, I speak these things. The one who sent me is with me. He does not leave me alone, because I always do the things which please him." (John 8:23-29)

I Am. Jesus meant more than just believing He existed. Unless you believe that I exist . . . misses the point. Jesus was more than just a man. He was the Son of God in the flesh. God had long been associated with that name: I Am. Remember Moses at the burning bush? *Then Moses said to God, "If I come to the people of Israel and say to them, 'The God of your fathers has sent me to you,' and they ask me, 'What is his name?' what shall I say to them?" God said to Moses, "I AM WHO I AM." And he said, "Say this to the people of Israel, 'I AM has sent me to you.'"* (Exodus 3:13–14) A similar description is used in Revelation: *I Am the Alpha and the Omega, who is and who was and who is to come, the Almighty.* (Revelation 1:8)

That's not a title. It's not a nickname. I AM is a statement of being. I AM emphasizes His present, eternal and unchanging nature. It is a name that belongs only to the One who stands before time, beyond time, and outside the limits of creation. That name belongs to the One who is self-existent and self-sustaining.

Before the Manger

The Word became flesh and made his dwelling among us. (John 1:14) From beginning to end the Gospels declare Jesus' unique character. Matthew and Luke begin with Jesus' birth. A child born to a virgin. The story seems too remarkable, almost unbelievable. It is contrary to the natural world. Whoever heard of such a thing? John begins his gospel before that. Before? What could come before Jesus' birth? *In the beginning was the Word, and the Word was with God, and the Word was God. He was with God in the beginning. Through him all things were made; without him nothing was made that has been made.* (John 1:1-3) Did you catch the significance of that? Jesus existed before the world was created. *In the beginning, God created the heavens and the earth.* (Genesis 1:1) Jesus was already there! He existed before Adam, Abraham, Moses, and David. *I tell you the truth,* Jesus answered, *before Abraham was, I Am!* (John 8:58) Jesus existed before God said *Let there be light!* and before the Spirit of God moved over the face of the waters. *Jesus Christ is the same yesterday, today, and forever.* (Hebrews 13:8) He didn't exist in physical, bodily form. He existed in the form of God.

The Creator Stepped Into His Creation

Jesus didn't just show up in the story. Jesus wrote the story. Not only did Jesus exist before the creation of the world, He created the world. He created everything you see, hear, or experience. Jesus was more than a great teacher, a great prophet, or a godly man. He was God. And, more than that, He is God. His birth was a miracle. His life was blameless. His resurrection was incomparable. He didn't arrive on the scene halfway through history. He laid the foundation of the world with His own hands.

At every point in Jesus' life, His deity shines like a light in a dark place. His birth was unique. His mother was a virgin. Mary wasn't just a young girl with a questionable pregnancy. Mary was a young woman who had never experienced sexual contact with a man. For a virgin to become pregnant was unfathomable. God's Son entered the world unlike any other.

Jesus lived a sinless life. He made not one mistake. He committed no error. He didn't tell a lie. He didn't deceive anyone. He didn't take advantage of anyone. He didn't cheat anyone. He didn't lust or covet. He wasn't greedy or self-centered. He wasn't any of the things I have been or you have been. He constantly walked in God's will. He was one with the Father. He was filled with the Spirit. He performed countless miracles. He fed the hungry. He gave sight to the blind. He helped the lame walk. He caused the mute to speak. He cast out demons with authority. He calmed storms with a word. He raised the dead with a whisper. He loved the people around Him. He saw the forgotten and lifted the broken. He spoke kindly to outcasts and treated everyone with respect and dignity. There has never been any other man like Him. Jesus wasn't just a man full of God. Jesus was God, full of grace and truth, walking among us in human flesh.

Perfect for the Imperfect

It was imperative that Jesus be perfect. Only a perfect, holy man could die for the sins of an imperfect, unholy people. Jesus offered Himself as the perfect Lamb of God for me, for you, for everyone.

It had to be Him. No one else could do it. No one else was qualified. No one else was clean. If Jesus had sinned—just once—He'd need saving too. But He didn't. Not in thought, not in word, not in deed. Not even for a second. He lived in perfect obedience with every step aligned with the will of the Father. That's what made Him the only worthy sacrifice. A sinner can't die for another sinner and expect to remove guilt. That's like trying to clean a window with muddy hands. It only smears the mess. But Jesus had no mud. He was the spotless Lamb of God.

Jesus fulfilled the promise. In the Old Testament, lambs without defect were offered. Sacrifices had to be flawless, untouched by disease or injury. Those lambs pointed forward to something greater. Someone greater. The Lamb who would take away the sin of the world—not just cover it temporarily, but remove it completely. Jesus didn't just **live** without sin. He **became** sin for us.

Let that land. *God made him who had no sin to be sin for us.* He took our place. He bore our guilt. He stood under the wrath we deserved.

And what do we get in return?

So that in Him we might become the righteousness of God. He didn't just take our punishment—He gave us His purity. He took the shame. We get the standing. He wore our sin. We wear His name.

That's the great exchange. The holy for the unholy. The perfect for the broken. All of it resting on the shoulders of one man—Jesus Christ. Only a perfect Savior could make imperfect people right with a perfect God. *God made Him who had no sin to be sin for us, so that in Him we might become the righteousness of God.* (2 Corinthians 5:21)

Jesus didn't stumble into death. He walked straight toward it. The cross wasn't a tragic end. It was the target. He died on the cross at the hands of sinful men. He intentionally came into the world to die on the cross. The cross was his mission. The cross was his purpose. Jesus came to bring salvation. He came to seek and save the lost. He came to die for sinners. He came to redeem and justify those who have faith in him.

He died—but not like any other man. His resurrection on the third day was the final proof, the divine vindication that declared Him the Son of God with power. *And who through the Spirit of holiness was declared with power to be the Son of God by his resurrection from the dead: Jesus Christ our Lord.* (Romans 1:4) Jesus rose from the grave on the third day. At least three times Jesus predicted His death and resurrection. Jesus' teaching was so well known the Pharisees asked for a guard to be stationed outside the tomb to prevent some type of fraud or hoax.

His exit from this world was as unique as His entrance. Even though there were other people who were resurrected, Jesus was unique and different. Elijah resurrected the son of the widow from Zarephath. Elisha resurrected the son of the Shunnamite woman. A dead man came back to life when he touched Elijah's bones. Jesus resurrected the widow of Nain's son, Jairus' daughter, and Lazarus. At the death of Jesus, many holy people were resurrected and appeared in Jerusalem. Peter raised Tabitha from the dead, and Paul raised Eutychus. All of those died again. However, Jesus' resurrection was eternal. He would never return to the grave. He was the firstfruits. He was the first of his kind. After 40 days of speaking with His disciples concerning the kingdom of God, He was taken up before their eyes into the clouds. Someday, he will return in the same way.

When He returns, mankind will be judged. Every human being will appear before God's judgment seat. Every human being will be assigned to heaven or hell. Every human being will receive reward or punishment. Every human being. God created mankind. God will judge mankind.

If you find it difficult to wrap your head around such a concept, welcome to the club. An immortal God wrapped Himself in mortal flesh. A God who knows no boundaries subjected Himself to space and time constraints. Jesus was born, lived, and died just like all of humanity. Yet, He was different. He was God's firstborn son. He was unique. He was one of a kind.

Every path to God isn't the same. There is only one path to God: Jesus Christ. Jesus was more than a prophet. Jesus is the Son of God.

That is the mystery of Jesus.

Who, being in very nature God, did not consider equality with God something to be grasped, but made himself nothing, taking the very nature of a servant, being made in human likeness. And being found in appearance as a man, he humbled himself and became obedient to death— even death on a cross!

Therefore God exalted him to the highest place and gave him the name that is above every name, that at the name of Jesus every knee should bow, in heaven and on earth and under the earth, and every tongue confess that Jesus Christ is Lord, to the glory of God the Father. (Philippians 2: 6-11)

Beyond all question, the mystery of godliness is great: He appeared in a body, was vindicated by the Spirit, was seen by angels, was preached among the nations, was believed on in the world, was taken up in glory. (1 Timothy 3:16)

Jesus died on the cross for your sin. The only path to forgiveness is through him. Jesus is the only avenue of forgiveness. Jesus is the only road to salvation. *I am the way, the truth, and the light. No one comes to the Father, except through me.* (John 14:6)

Jesus didn't die to make salvation possible. He died to make it certain—for those who believe.

There is only one road that leads to life: Jesus Christ. It isn't found through a moral lifestyle or through sincere intentions. The way isn't hidden. God didn't make it complicated. It's not cruel. It's kind. Because in a world of dead ends and detours, Jesus draws you a map—and then becomes the road.

The cross wasn't a random tragedy or a cruel twist of history. It was the deliberate outpouring of divine love. Jesus did not die for an abstract idea or a general notion of wrongdoing. He died for your sin. Jesus didn't die for vague, theoretical sin. He died for your sin. He bore your pride, your deceit, your bitterness, your hidden wounds, and your deepest shame. Every offense was placed upon Him, and every burden was carried to the place of execution. On a wooden beam outside the walls of Jerusalem, the Son of God took upon Himself the penalty that belonged to you, so that you might receive the life that belonged to Him.

And then He walked out of the grave. Alive. Triumphant. Still bearing the scars that bought your peace.

So what now?

The first step of your journey is to believe Jesus is who he said He was: God's firstborn son, the Lamb of God, the atonement for your sin, the firstfruits of the resurrection, the Savior of the world.

Don't just believe He existed. Believe He's **everything**. Because when you finally realize who the Driver is, you stop looking for the next signpost. You stop asking for shortcuts. You stop wondering if you've gone too far to turn around.

The Road Ahead

If Jesus is the destination, grace is the on-ramp. Everything begins with Him. But nothing moves forward without grace. You can know who Jesus is. You can even believe He's the Son of God. But until you understand **why** He came—until you grasp what His death accomplished—you're still standing on the side of the road, looking at the car but never stepping in.

Grace is not a reward for the strong. It's not a prize for the righteous. Grace flows from the heart of God to the undeserving, the broken, the sinful—and yes, the good people who never knew they were lost. Grace rewrites the story. It unchains the prisoner. It silences the accuser. It takes the shame you've buried deep and lifts it to the light.

Grace is not leniency. It is not passive. It is fierce, holy love in motion—poured out through the blood of Jesus. It is God's favor resting on those who have no résumé, no defense, no excuse. It is the only reason any of us have hope. You don't earn grace. You receive it. And once you do, nothing stays the same.

In the next chapter, we'll step into that grace. We'll explore what it really means to be saved by it, changed by it, and fueled by it. Because the road to salvation doesn't just require a Savior—it requires the gift only He can give.

And that gift...
is grace.

Grace

The Key Was Turned Before You Got In

He had rehearsed the speech in his mind a hundred times. Each word shaped by regret. Each sentence soaked in shame. "I am no longer worthy to be called your son. Just make me like one of your hired servants." The road home stretched longer than he remembered, and the weight of his failure grew heavier with every step. The smell of the pigs still clung to his clothes. The consequences of his choices had etched lines on his face and sorrow into his heart. He had wasted his time, money, and talent. He headed back home broke and ashamed. He didn't expect restoration. He only hoped for survival.

But while he was still a long way off, his father saw him. And the father ran.

The Father didn't run because he was surprised or because he needed answers. He didn't ask a thousand condemning, probing questions. He didn't run because his son deserved it. He ran because he loved. In spite of everything that had happened, the prodigal was still his son. The father didn't wait for an apology. He didn't demand a record of wrongdoing. That father ran and threw his arms around the filth, the smell, the failure, and the wreckage.

That is what grace looks like.

The father didn't ask about the squandered money. He called for a robe. He called for a ring. He called for a feast. He rejoiced! The son expected condemnation. The son knew he deserved condemnation. He received celebration. He prepared for rejection. He found restoration.

That is the grace of God.

Grace doesn't wait for worthiness. It doesn't respond to performance. It moves first. It covers shame. It replaces disgrace with honor. It throws a party where we expect a penalty. And it welcomes us home with the full weight of the Father's joy.

This chapter is about that grace. The kind that runs toward you while you're still in the distance. The kind that embraces before you explain. The kind that restores what was broken and calls it whole again. Grace does not make sense to the world. But it is the very heart of God.

Grace is the moment the key turns. The engine doesn't roar to life because you provided spark, fuel, and oxygen. It starts because God wanted it to start. Grace isn't the reward you get after a long, uphill climb. It's the reason you're even on the road.

When the Engine Turns Before You Touch the Keys

Salvation begins and ends with God's grace. Without God's action, there is nothing. The universe would not exist, the earth would not exist, humanity would not exist, and you would not exist. Without God's grace, nothing would exist.

Most imagine grace as a pat on the back for trying. A cosmic nod from God saying, "Good effort." But grace has never been God meeting you halfway. He doesn't wait on the porch tapping His foot. He runs to you. Sandals flying. Arms wide.

Without grace, there's no ignition. No spark. No fuel. No oxygen. You don't move an inch. Grace is what gets the wheels turning. It's the voice that says, "You don't deserve this, but I'm giving it to you anyway."

But grace gets misunderstood all the time. Some think it's cheap. Some imagine it only applies to the cleaned-up, not the messed-up. It's neither of those.

This chapter is about clearing the fog. Grace isn't something you climb up to. It's what reaches down to you. It's the hand that finds yours in the dark. The story starts with grace. The story ends with grace. It always has.

Running on Empty Trying To Earn It

Some people treat grace like a paycheck. Do enough good, keep your nose clean, follow the rules—then maybe, just maybe, God cuts you a check with heaven written on it. So they hustle. They behave. They polish their Sunday smiles and try to act like they've got it all together. They believe salvation's for the squeaky-clean. For the ones who don't drink, don't curse, don't mess up. And if they're honest, deep down they think they've got to earn love. God's love is nice, but it feels like something that needs to be deserved. So they live with this low-grade anxiety that they're never quite enough. That they've still got more to prove. That one wrong move might send everything crashing. For them, grace is like a treadmill. You sweat and strain, but you never arrive.

How does one explain the grace of God? How can we make sense of it? Humanity desires to make itself the center of existence. How can it comprehend that One greater provides everything? We want to determine we are worthy of God's grace. Yet, in doing so, we nullify God's grace. If we are worthy or we earn it, it isn't grace. If you could work your way into God's favor, Jesus would not have needed to die for you.

Man has always struggled to understand God's grace. Grace astounds and challenges our rationale. God chooses to save. Simply put, that is what grace means. God chose to provide a means of forgiveness. God chose to provide an atonement for your sin. God chooses not to count your sin against you through faith in Jesus. God chooses to give you eternal life.

Sin isn't a surface wound. It's not a paper cut you patch with a few good deeds. Sin breaks. It fractures the relationship with God so deeply that no amount of trying can put the pieces back. You can't work your way back from a chasm. That's why grace doesn't meet you halfway. It comes all the way because you can't reach at all.

Pride hates that. Pride whispers, "You're close. You've almost got it. Just a little more effort, and you'll be good enough." Grace shuts that down. Grace says, "You're not good enough. But I love you anyway."

And here's the part that flips everything: God didn't have to save you. He chose to. He's not obligated to forgive you. He wants to. That's grace. Grace isn't a transaction. Grace is a gift.

Start seeing grace for what it is—a decision God made before you ever took a breath. He didn't look at your potential. He didn't wait to see if you'd get your act together. He acted first. Grace was never a reward for good behavior. It was always a rescue mission.

Stop measuring your worth by your performance. Stop thinking God's approval is something to chase. Grace doesn't care how polished you look or how many rules you follow. It doesn't wait for you to impress. It meets you in the ditch and throws open the passenger door.

Jesus is the only reason you're even in the car. Without Him, you're not just lost—you're not even on the map. Grace isn't Jesus giving you a boost. Grace is Jesus carrying you the whole way.

God doesn't owe you anything. That truth stings, but it sets you free. You don't have to earn what's already been given. You don't have to keep performing to stay loved.

That's the scandal of grace. Grace doesn't wait for worthiness. Grace doesn't respond to goodness. It moves first. And it never looks back.

A great question to ask is "Why is grace even necessary?"

God Started It All

Some believe the world is the result of a cosmic explosion. If something exploded or something went "bang," from where did it originate? From where did it come? Something or someone has to be the eternal component, the thing that always exists. The eternal component is God. This isn't designed to be a scientific explanation. I am neither qualified nor smart enough to give a scientific statement. I am a theologian, not a scientist. Yet, my faith in creation isn't unfounded. I need a more plausible and believable explanation than God to change my mind. I am opinionated because of my faith in God. That I do not deny. Yet, evolution doesn't persuade me as a more viable option. In fact, the prospect that this life is the totality of our existence is a dismal thought.

We exist by God's grace. You're here because God wanted you here. Life wasn't a random bang. It was a gift. Grace didn't begin at the cross—it began with *in the beginning God created the heavens and the earth*. For you, it began with your first breath. Life is the result of God's grace. It is God's gift. You didn't cause yourself. You didn't build the world. You showed up in the middle of a story already unfolding. God wasn't forced to create you. Nobody twisted His arm. You weren't even around to make a case for your existence. God chose to do it. God created humanity, and you, out of love. That's grace.

The same God who created you chose to save you. Again—unforced. Again—unearned. Salvation, like creation, starts with grace. You didn't climb up to Him. He came down to you. You didn't negotiate for a second chance. He offered one before you knew you needed it. Simply put, grace is God for you.

Too many people shrink the Gospel into a clean equation. Man sinned. God got angry. Jesus stepped in. That's not wrong, but it's way too thin. Grace isn't math. It's more like music—something that hits deeper than logic and lingers longer than words. God wasn't surprised when Adam and Eve sinned. Before God created the world, salvation by grace through faith in Jesus was the plan. Jesus was not Plan B. Jesus was Plan A from the very beginning. Astounding! The plan of salvation was in place before the creation of the world. God's grace.

God created mankind. Then, God gave mankind a choice. And mankind chose to rebel. One command, one tree in the middle of the garden, and Adam and Eve couldn't resist. Don't be too critical. You would have done the same thing. As the result of Adam and Eve's choice, sin entered the world. Sin brought death and punishment.

Sin separated man from God. And once our sin separates, we have no avenue to repair our broken relationship. A hundred, or even a thousand, good things won't restore the relationship. When it's broken, it's broken. There is no spiritual superglue for a quick fix. Sin separates us from God. Every time, without exception. God didn't bend His own rules to get you off the hook. He honored them. He satisfied them. He didn't ignore justice. He fulfilled it with blood.

Yet, it is more complicated than it sounds. God dealt with sin in a way that doesn't violate His nature. Sin demands justice. Real justice. God's justice demands sin must be punished. God cannot dismiss sin without a penalty. When someone suffers a wrong, he usually wants the offending person punished. He wants justice. When someone wrongs another, he usually wants mercy. We see that in court cases and lawsuits every day. It's human nature.

We want God to casually dismiss our sin, but God's justice doesn't allow God to wink at sin. It is serious. It is wrong. It is against God's nature. It makes God's nostrils flare in anger. You must pay for your sin. Yet, you have nothing to offer. You are without hope.

That is the problem. You are guilty. You stand before God with nothing to offer. You possess no righteousness to exchange for mercy. You have no defense to justify your condition. You cannot present a single reason why grace should be extended to you. Your hands are empty, and your debt is beyond repayment.

Enter Jesus. Jesus became the atoning sacrifice for our sin. *God made him who had no sin to become sin for us, so that in him we might become the righteousness of God.* Jesus was necessary because of God's justice. As a just judge, God requires punishment for sin. Only Jesus, the Sinless One, can offer such a gift. Jesus died for your sin. He took your place. Without Jesus, only death was possible. He freely took your place. God freely sent His Son. You didn't deserve it. Jesus chose to sacrifice Himself to atone for your sin. God's grace. Without Jesus' atoning sacrifice, there can be no peace with God. Grace means God loved us and sent His Son to be the propitiation for our sin.

Never forget that God had two options. One was to save. The second was to destroy. God, in His anger, could destroy. And in doing so, God would be just. God chose not to. God chose to save. God chose to restore our broken relationship. God chose to send Jesus. *For God so loved the world that He sent His one and only Son that whoever believes in Him might not perish, but might have eternal life.* (John 3:16) God's grace.

We were not worthy of Jesus. We did nothing to justify His coming. We weren't on the cusp of being good. God sent His Son while we were sinners. God sent His Son when we had no hope. God sent His Son because we were evil. God sent His Son because we rebelled against Him. God isn't obligated to offer you salvation. He doesn't owe it to you. His love necessitates His grace. Every spiritual blessing available to you results from God's grace.

Several years ago, our oldest son, Houston, was on his way to begin an internship with the Shiner Church of Christ in Williamsburg, Kentucky. Just north of Nashville, as he traveled along I-65, he struck a pothole that was anything but ordinary. The impact destroyed his tire and bent the wheel. The trip stopped right there on the shoulder. It wasn't just inconvenient. It was costly. It did more than interrupt a trip. It caused damage that had to be addressed before he could move forward.

That's how it is on the road to salvation. There are potholes. They aren't little distractions or minor detours. These are deep enough to damage your journey if you're not watching. Not every obstacle comes with flashing lights and warning signs. Some lie beneath the surface, waiting for the right moment to throw everything off course. Some are obvious. Others are hidden until the impact rattles your faith.

Potholes

Pride

Pride is one of the largest and most dangerous.

Pride convinces a person that grace is unnecessary. It whispers that you are strong enough, capable enough, and righteous enough to reach the destination on your own. It causes you to resist what you cannot control and reject what you cannot earn. Pride creates the illusion that salvation is owed rather than offered.

Pride doesn't scream. Pride whispers, "You've got this." Pride tells you to grip the wheel tighter, mash the gas harder, and prove your worth every mile. Pride doesn't need help. Pride draws its own map. Pride wants to pull into heaven with its own horsepower.

Pride challenges our acceptance of God's grace. We want to feel that we earned it. That somehow, we confirm or validate the gift God offers.

Pride causes grace to become offensive. Grace doesn't need your effort. Grace doesn't read your résumé. Grace makes you admit you are not enough. And that stings.

We don't want a gift. We want a paycheck. We want to feel like we earned it. We want to believe we deserved it. We want to think God saw something in us that deserved saving. But that isn't how grace works. Grace isn't a bonus for the well-behaved. It is rescue for the rebellious.

It's one of the most dangerous potholes because it feels noble. Pride says, "I just need a little help." Grace says, "You are powerless without me." Pride wants a partner. Grace wants surrender.

Humility levels the road. A humble heart recognizes its dependence on God. That is one of the most freeing and enlightening truths in this world. For everything, you are dependent on God. Pride creates a need to achieve and to earn. Humility creates dependence on a gracious, loving, and kind God.

Legalism

Grace scares rule-keepers. Grace creates freedom. Legalism demands limits. Legalism seeks proof. It respects performance. It wants a system where you always know what to do. It tracks how well you did. And it keeps score. Legalism turns faith into a spreadsheet. If your math adds up, you are good. If it doesn't, you're out.

Legalism math works like this: Try harder + Do more + Earn your place = SALVATION. But grace doesn't add up.

Grace isn't a calculation. It is a gift. A gift doesn't reward effort. It replaces effort. The real danger of legalism isn't exhaustion. The real danger is delusion. You think you are making changes because you are checking boxes. But deep down, nothing is changing.

Grace invites transformation, not performance. Legalism thinks grace is soft. It sees grace as reckless. Legalism thinks grace is dangerous, so it slows you down with fear, guilt, and pressure. When you understand grace, you don't want to run wild. You want to run home.

Shame

Shame convinces us there is a road to God, but that it isn't for people like us. You know grace exists. You know the verses. You've seen the cross. You listened to the sermons. But deep down, you believe there is a limit, and that you crossed it a long time ago. It manifests itself in statements like "If you knew what I've done." "God could never forgive someone like me." "Some sins are too dark to be washed clean." "God loves people, but not people like me."

That's how shame works. It whispers that you are too dirty, too broken, too stained. It convinces you that grace has boundaries. Shame turns the gospel into good news for other people.

You find the perfect car and make an offer. The salesman promises the price, shakes your hand, and asks you to step into his office. He says, "Let me check with my sales manager. I'm sure there won't be a problem. Congratulations."

Then, he comes back with a nervous laugh and says, "Sorry. I can't do that after all. My numbers didn't reflect our true inventory cost."

The offer's gone. The handshake meant nothing. Turns out, the deal was only good until he knew the full story.

That's how a lot of people think grace works. Like God made the offer too soon. Before He knew who you really were. Before He saw the things you've done, the things you still struggle with, and the thoughts you don't say out loud.

You assume once He sees the whole picture, He'll pull the offer back. Revoke His grace. Withdraw His love. Deny access to forgiveness.

But God doesn't work like that.

He knew exactly who you were before He made the offer. He knew every secret, every failure. He saw every moment you hoped no one else saw. And He sent Jesus anyway.

The deal still stands. Not because you're good. Because He is.

Satan: When The Enemy Becomes Your Inner Voice

Satan's greatest work happens in silence. Satan doesn't need to tempt you to do something wild. He just needs to convince you that you aren't worth saving.

He waits. He waits for the silence. The moment after you sin. The second before you pray. The quiet place where you are the most vulnerable. Then He whispers. "You aren't really forgiven." "You aren't like other Christians." "You're the only one who struggles."

The worst part is that it sounds like your own voice. It doesn't sound like an attack. It resonates as honesty. You think you are just telling yourself the hard truth. That you are acknowledging reality.

He slides into your mind, holds up a mirror, and distorts the image until all you can see are your flaws. Your weaknesses shine like the sun. Your worst days flood your mind. You don't see the healing power of grace in the cracks of your life.

You start comparing. You think of someone who knows more Scripture. You see someone with rock-like faith who never seems to waver. You see someone who worships with joy and never misses a Sunday. You compare your hidden wounds to their polished exterior. You stack your shame against their smile. And you think, "They belong here. I don't."

Satan loves that. He loves to make grace feel like it is for other people. The devil doesn't need you to run from God. He just needs to convince you that God would never run toward you. Satan wants you to see God as tired and disappointed with you. Satan wants you to think grace is limited, and you've already used up your part. That, the next time you mess up, it's over. Satan is the Accuser. His best accusing happens in the quiet places of your mind.

But here's the truth. God isn't holding His breath waiting to be disappointed. God wants to rescue you from self-doubt.

God isn't keeping secret tabs on all your mistakes. God is erasing them by the blood of Jesus. Satan's lies accuse you of being unworthy. God calls you redeemed in Jesus. Don't let the voice in your head speak louder than the truth of the cross.

Through the Eyes of Grace

What does God see when He looks at you? God sees the real you.

God sees you with doubts and scars. He knows the stories you hope no one ever finds out. He sees the one who wrestles with guilt and sinks into doubt. God sees that. But He also sees more. God sees the version you don't believe is even possible. He sees the version of you washed clean by the blood of His Son.

He also sees the polished version. The cleaned-up, Sunday-best, say-the-right-thing, and do-the-right-thing version. Yes, God knows everything: every secret, every stumble, every sin. But God also sees you as spotless: without blemish, without fault, without sin. Not because you lived perfectly — because Jesus did. When God looks at you through grace, He doesn't see the stain. He sees the sacrifice.

Grace changes the lens. God doesn't view you through your failures. He views you through the finished work of the cross. The blood of Jesus doesn't smudge the truth—it rewrites it.

Not because you earned it. Because He gave it.

Not because you're impressive. Because He is.

Grace doesn't ignore who you've been. It transforms who you are.

And when you finally believe that—when you start seeing yourself through His eyes—everything changes.

You didn't do anything to cause God to offer it. He didn't give it because you asked the right way or scored high enough on some invisible scale. It wasn't a reward. It was a rescue. An unprovoked act of outrageous love.

Grace was God's initiative. He made the first move. Not because you were almost there, but because you had no way to get there. You weren't worthy. Your résumé didn't qualify you. Your behavior didn't recommend you. Your reputation didn't help your case. You weren't close. You weren't even asking.

And still, He came.

Jesus did not enter the world by accident. His coming was not a reaction to failure or an emergency response to sin. It was a declaration spoken from eternity into time. Grace is the heart of God revealed. It is God acting on your behalf, not from obligation, but from love. The cross was not a correction to a broken plan. It was the plan. Long before the garden. Long before the fall. Long before the dust was formed into man and breath filled his lungs. You were already in the mind of God. You were already held in His heart.

What, then, is your worth? What is your value?

It is the arrival of God in the flesh. It is the blood of the Son poured out for your redemption. It is the grace of the Father offered freely for your salvation. That is your value. If you miss it, you miss the very thing for which God put breath in your nostrils.

So what does God see?

He sees one He died to save. He sees one He longs to redeem. He sees one He has not forgotten, not abandoned, and not given up on. Even now, after all that has been done, after all the wandering, after all the silence and shame and sorrow, He still wants you.

Grace is God saying, I see it all. And I'm not leaving.

That's what you're worth.

It is not found in what you have done. It is found in what He has done for you. It is measured not by your achievements or failures, but by the price He was willing to pay. And He paid with everything.

Don't mistake undeserved for unconditional. Grace is a gift, but it is not automatic. It must be received. It must be embraced by faith. Not everyone chooses to respond. For those who do, grace is waiting. And the arms of God are still open.

For you are saved by grace through faith.

The offer is real. And it's personal. And it's yours.

The Road Ahead

Grace opens the door. Faith steps through it. You didn't earn God's grace. You didn't deserve it. But now that it's been offered, what will you do with it? Grace is God handing you the keys. Faith is turning the ignition.

Faith isn't a feeling. It's not a warm thought or spiritual optimism. Faith is trust that moves your feet. It's belief that changes your direction. It's confidence not in yourself, but in the One who died for you. Grace made the way. Faith walks it.

The next chapter isn't about trying harder. It's about trusting deeper. We'll look at what real, saving faith looks like—not just belief in your head, but surrender in your heart. Because if grace is the voice that says, "You're mine," then faith is the voice that answers, "Yes, Lord. I'm yours."

Let's turn the key. Let's move. Let's talk about faith.

Faith: Pressing the Pedal

Saying Yes to the Journey

You are saved by grace through faith . . .

Several years ago, DiAnne and I visited Mykonos. It's a beautiful place—bright white buildings, blue roofs, cobblestone alleys. But what surprised me most were the streets. They were unbelievably narrow. If a vehicle came down the street, we had no choice but to step into the doorway of a nearby shop and wait for it to pass. And standing there, tucked into the threshold of a shop, I heard Jesus' words echo in my spirit: *But small is the gate and narrow is the road that leads to life, and only a few find it.* (Matthew 7:14)

That verse took on a whole new meaning. Suddenly, it didn't feel abstract. It felt literal. The narrow road isn't spacious or easy. It's tight. It's uncomfortable. It forces you to choose—to be alert, to move with purpose, to watch your step. That means not everyone finds it. Not everyone wants it. And not everyone is willing to walk it.

The narrow road Jesus spoke of isn't just a metaphor. It's a movement. It's a direction and a way of walking through the world that feels increasingly out of step with everything around us. The road is called faith. Faith isn't a vague belief or some type of cultural Christianity. Faith moves your feet and shapes your life.

This chapter is about that kind of faith.

Faith?

"Am I a believer?" "Do I have faith in Jesus?" Do you ever find yourself pondering those questions? How does one know if he has faith? How can one truly determine if he possesses genuine faith? What does faith actually encompass, and how can we recognize its presence?

Every day, we meet people who say they believe in Jesus. Some live in a way that looks holy. Some talk like disciples, serve in churches, and post Bible verses on social media accounts. Others seem half-hearted, inconsistent, or even worse, hypocritical.

But here's the truth—we don't know what's happening in someone's soul. It's crucial to remember that it is not our role to pass judgment. We can't see what God sees. God's all-seeing gaze delves deep into the very core of our beings. No action, thought, motive, or underlying reason is hidden from His omniscient sight.

We should never assume that someone's faith is weak or strong based on our limited understanding. The loudest and most apparent faith isn't always the strongest. Those we think have rock-solid faith may be barely hanging on through their hidden struggles. Those who seem to have weak faith may be the ones clinging to Jesus with the fiercest, most unshakable faith of all.

The Wide Road

The spiritual road we must travel is much different than most people think it is. It's not a wide, easy super-highway leading to a carefree existence. Jesus warned us about this misconception and advised us to take a different path. He said, *Enter through the narrow gate. For wide is the gate and broad is the road that leads to destruction. But small is the gate and narrow is the road that leads to life, and only a few find it.* (Matthew 7:13-14)

The superhighway is packed. It's wide, smooth, and fast. It stretches across life's landscape, gleaming with promises and pulsing with motion. It looks like it is going somewhere. It looks like progress. It looks like success. It gives the impression everyone finally figured out where they are going.

If you look closely, you will see two lanes, side by side, both full, both moving at breakneck speed. Both lanes are headed somewhere. Both lanes are full of people who think they are on the right road. The lanes are full of atheists and believers, obedient and rebellious, churchgoers and skeptics, rule-breakers and rule-keepers. Some are wildly immoral; some are radically moral. Different motives, Different methods. But headed to the same destination. Destruction.

One lane speeds ahead with no thought of God at all. No reverence. No accountability. It powers on by self-made success and self-defined truth. It is the lane of "follow your heart," "you do you," and "whatever makes me happy." It brims with freedom on the surface. It grabs the gusto of the world. It analyzes existence only by the time we spend on this earth. It is self-centered, self-promoting, and self-absorbed. It grabs life by the horns and rides the bull for all it is worth.

The other lane is far more subtle. And far more dangerous. It has church signs, worship music, and moral behavior. It seeks God's blessings, His comfort, and His protection. But, not His presence. Not His lordship. It's a version of faith that wants the crown without the cross. It prays for miracles but avoids surrender. It uses God as a means to an end but never bows in trust. It might look like faith, but it's not faith. It looks more holy than the other lane, but it promises happiness without holiness.

The lanes look drastically different, but they are headed to the same destination. Destruction.

The Narrow Road

Jesus' way is the dirt path — rugged, weathered, narrow, and winding. It's not paved with convenience, lined with neon signs, or lit by the glow of popularity. It snakes through deep valleys and climbs rugged mountains. It crosses rivers that can sweep you off your feet and deserts that burn your endurance raw. It walks through quiet, peaceful lush forests and briar patches that tear at your skin. Jesus' road is the kind shepherds traveled, not kings. It the footpath of exiles, not the star-studded walks of celebrities. It's more boots-in-the-mud than loafers-on-the-desk. It's the kind of path you don't find on the map. You find it by following the voice that says, *Come, follow me.*

When you answer that call in faith, God's grace rushes in. Grace doesn't hesitate. It wraps around you like sunlight after the storm and water in the desert. Grace is vast. It is wide enough for the world and deep enough for every failure. God's grace can cover every sinner from Eden to eternity. God's grace isn't inadequate. It's an overflowing abundance that can cleanse and heal us.

But grace isn't automatic. It's available to all, but poured out on those who believe. *We are saved by grace through faith.* (Ephesians 2:8)

Faith Isn't Flashy

Since we are *saved by grace through faith*, we should desperately want to know what faith is. We want to know we have faith. We want confidence. We don't want some wishy-washy hope so. We crave a strong, unwavering confidence in our faith. Sometimes we compare ourselves to biblical figures who showed remarkable faith. In doing so, we convince ourselves that we could never measure up. But I want to emphasize that God's call to faith in Jesus is not about doing amazing things. It's not about things like parting seas or walking on water. God doesn't expect you to heal a sick person or cleanse a leper. He doesn't expect you to destroy the walls of Jericho or be thrown into a lions' den. Those stories are awe-inspiring. They are great testaments of faith. But God works an even greater miracle in each of us.

Faith in Jesus provides the power to shape and mold us into the individuals God intended us to be. It is in this deep faith that we can discover true contentment, experience lasting peace, and find our ultimate purpose. Faith in Jesus does not require us to perform miracles or achieve monumental accomplishments. It is about a genuine and unwavering trust in His guidance, love, and grace. By placing our faith in Jesus, we embark on a journey of personal growth and fulfillment that far surpasses anything we could ever imagine.

How do we have that faith? That is the issue. Our faith is what limits us, what holds us back from fully experiencing the blessings of God's grace. Faith is not something easily obtained. Faith is a rare and precious commodity. But it is something that God desires for everyone to possess. He wants us to trust in Him wholeheartedly, to have faith in His goodness and love. We can overcome any obstacle with genuine faith. We can also experience the full life God planned for us.

False Faith and Hidden Pride

What does that faith look like? Let's look at a couple of negative examples.

In Jesus' day, the Pharisees had every appearance of religious devotion. They gained widespread recognition for their pious practices. They prayed, fasted, and read their Bibles. They kept separate from unrighteous people. They were full of piety and devotion. In today's society, the majority of churches would eagerly embrace such committed individuals with unwavering religious zeal. Most churches would welcome them in with exuberance and thankfulness. However, it is important to note that Jesus openly rebuked and condemned them. He labeled them "white-washed tombs," "hypocrites," and "blind guides." We find ourselves fervently desiring to avoid falling into that same category. We don't aspire to just look righteous. We want to *be* righteous.

"Not everyone who says to me, 'Lord, Lord,' will enter the kingdom of heaven, but only he who does the will of my Father who is in heaven. Many will say to me on that day, 'Lord, Lord, did we not prophesy in your name, and in your name drive out demons and perform many miracles?' Then I will tell them plainly, 'I never knew you. Away from me, you evildoers!"(Matthew 7:21–23)

Frightening, isn't it? Jesus alludes to a person who sincerely believed he was fulfilling his purpose. He thought he was doing the right thing. The type of person who goes to church every Sunday. The type of person who serves in what seems like great ways with great enthusiasm. Jesus' statement doesn't describe someone who is "sitting on the bench." Jesus describes a person who is "in the game." Jesus describes someone who is fully engaged. Someone actively striving to make a difference.

When we combine Jesus' words with the reality that we tend to think the very best of ourselves, we realize the need for honest self-evaluation. I can easily distort my perception of my own character. It is imperative that faith goes beyond mere verbal affirmation of belief in Jesus.

We must delve into a deep question: How does God define and measure true faith? Did you notice how Jesus defined the answer? *He who does the will of my Father who is in heaven.*

Empty Words vs. Living Faith

During His ministry, Jesus encountered demons who knew His identity. In Capernaum, Jesus encountered a man possessed by a demon, an evil spirit, in the synagogue. *And the demon shouted, "Ha! What do you want with us, Jesus of Nazareth? Have you come to destroy us? I know who you are—the Holy One of God!"* (Luke 4:34)

This incident serves as a captivating testament to Jesus' power and authority. His divine presence was so overwhelming that even the demons could not help but acknowledge who He was. This account surely leaves no room for doubt regarding the extraordinary nature of Jesus' ministry and His divine status as the Holy One of God.

James wrote, *You believe that there is one God. Good! Even the demons believe that—and shudder.* (James 2:19) James wants us to understand that mere belief, without any corresponding actions, is meaningless. It holds no weight, no purpose. It's like empty words spoken into the void. True faith is dynamic and transformative. It goes beyond acknowledging that Jesus is the Son of God. It is manifested in tangible actions that align with the will of God. Faith springs to life when we actively live out our beliefs. Don't settle for a faith that is stagnant, lifeless, and fruitless. Let your faith demonstrate its authenticity through your deeds. Let it be a manifestation of your dedication to honor and fulfill the will of God. After all, isn't that what genuine faith is all about?

Faith is more than a statement. Faith is more than a simple acknowledgment. That is part of faith, but that is not all of faith.

Let's look at a couple of positive examples.

A young Jewish man hung on a cross. He had done nothing wrong. He was the target of spiteful religious leaders consumed by hypocrisy and jealousy. They desired nothing more than to rid themselves of Him. His teachings had exposed their flawed interpretations of sacred Scripture. Jesus did not conform to their expectations. He boldly proclaimed He was the Messiah. But Jesus of Nazareth didn't fit their mold.

A young Jewish man hung on a cross. He had done nothing wrong, but He was doing everything right. Jesus of Nazareth wasn't on the cross by accident. He wasn't just a miscarriage of justice or a cruel twist of fate. Jesus of Nazareth was on that cross by design. He was fulfilling a divine plan made by God Himself. Jesus of Nazareth hung on the cross intentionally. That's right. Intentionally. It was God's plan for Jesus of Nazareth to hang on that cross. And Jesus of Nazareth always followed God's plan. That is faith.

Imagine the unwavering faith that brought Him to that cross. He knew full well the suffering and torment He would endure. Jesus followed God's plan faithfully. He did so even unto death because He understood the greater purpose behind His sacrifice. His selfless act made redemption and salvation possible for all people. This is no mere tale of justice denied; instead, it is a testament to God's grand design. For Jesus of Nazareth was not just another victim. He was the embodiment of unwavering faith. He fulfilled a divine plan that would change history forever.

The Criminal and Faith

Two criminals hung beside him. One hurled taunting and disrespectful words: "Aren't you the Christ? Save yourself and us!" The other criminal was overwhelmed by reverence. He shifted his gaze towards Jesus and scolded his companion. *We are punished justly, for we are getting what our deeds deserve. But this man has done nothing wrong. Jesus, remember me when you come into your kingdom.*

Did you get that? A criminal, hanging on a cross, moments before his death, anticipated Jesus as King. How could a young Jewish man, hanging on a cross, minutes or hours from death become King? That is faith.

Jesus emphatically responded to the criminal. He assured him, without a doubt, *Today, you will be with me in Paradise.*

Do you have the faith for that request? Jesus, remember me when you come into your kingdom. Jesus, be my King.

Did the criminal repent? The text doesn't explicitly say it, but his words point toward genuine remorse. Did he confess? *Jesus remember me when you come into your kingdom.* Sounds like it. Was he baptized? There was nothing to be baptized into yet. The criminal had no chance to be baptized traditionally. But, it's worth noting that baptism symbolizes uniting with Jesus in his death, burial, and resurrection. These transformative events had not yet occurred at the given moment in the text. Therefore, it is understandable why baptism may not have been applicable.

The words spoken by Jesus Himself offer great assurance. When He told the criminal, *Today you will be with me in Paradise*, it is an undeniable display of His authority and power. And Jesus has the authority to make that decision. Such divine guarantees should not be taken lightly.

The thief on the cross believed. He had faith at a time when most of those closest to Jesus were grappling with doubts and lack of faith.

Faith is not something we "do" to make ourselves acceptable to God. No human effort can attain that. If it could, the strong would boast in their abilities and despise those who lacked that ability. The weak would drown in their shame. Since salvation is a gift, there is no place for anyone to boast in their abilities. Everyone is on equal footing.

We all come to God empty-handed. No one climbs their way into grace. No one gets a head start because of spiritual talent. We stand on equal ground—at the foot of the cross, held up by mercy, not muscle. So there's no room for pride. No platform for performance. Only praise—for the God who gives what we could never deserve.

Abraham and Faith

After this, the word of the LORD came to Abram in a vision: *Do not be afraid, Abram. I am your shield, your very great reward." But Abram said, "O Sovereign LORD, what can you give me since I remain childless and the one who will inherit my estate is Eliezer of Damascus?" And Abram said, "You have given me no children; so a servant in my household will be my heir." Then the word of the LORD came to him: "This man will not be your heir, but a son coming from your own body will be your heir." He took him outside and said, "Look up at the heavens and count the stars—if indeed you can count them." Then he said to him, "So shall your offspring be." Abram believed the LORD, and he credited it to him as righteousness.* (Gen. 15:1–6)

Abraham believed God. Then, Abraham continued to believe God. Abraham had already responded to God's call to go to Canaan. Abraham trusted God. Abraham stood firm on God's promise. We know that Abraham was between 75 and 86 years old when God made this promise. 75 years with no child. And Abraham trusted God. Abraham trusted God to do the impossible. And it was credited to him as righteousness, but not because of his works. Abraham didn't earn it. Abraham received the promise through faith.

Both Paul and James quote that verse. *Abraham believed God and it was credited to him as righteousness.* Paul quotes it twice. James quotes it once. So it must be a very important verse. Yet, they use it in slightly different ways.

Paul writes, *What then shall we say that Abraham, our forefather, discovered in this matter? If, in fact, Abraham was justified by works, he has something to boast about – but not before God. What does the Scripture say? "Abraham believed God, and it was credited to him as righteousness."*

Here is my point. Meritorious works did not obligate God to bless Abraham. God didn't look down from heaven and say, "Well, that Abraham fellow is a rule-keeping guy. He's forced me to do something good for him. I'll give him a son." Abraham's rule-keeping didn't obligate God. God pronounced a blessing on Abraham, and Abraham considered it as good as done.

God pronounced a blessing on you: forgiveness of sin, eternal life, fellowship with God. You didn't earn it. It is not a wage, a payment for a job well done. It is a gift of God. God didn't look down from heaven and say, "You are such a good rule-keeping person. I'm obligated to do something for you. I'll just grant you eternal life." No, God saved you out of your sin, not because of your righteousness.

James highlighted the key mix of faith and deeds in Abraham's life. He stressed their true unity. Abraham didn't believe one thing and act in opposition to it. Abraham's faith and Abraham's works were consistent. Abraham exemplified how faith generates faithful actions by consistently aligning his faith with his works. Faith produces faithful works. The same is true for us. If you believe in Jesus, if you have faith, your works will be consistent with faith. Your faith will impact your behavior. Your deeds will testify to the genuineness of your faith.

So, where does that leave you today?

By grace, you are saved through faith – and this is not from yourselves, it is the gift of God – not by works so that no one may boast. (Ephesians 2:8-9)

God's plan for salvation is simple. It isn't changed by culture or human innovation. It doesn't depend on intellect or deep spiritual insight. Salvation is solely dependent on God's power and God's goodwill. By grace, God sent Jesus into this dark, sinful world to atone for your sin. You didn't deserve God's gift. You didn't earn God's gift. When you were trapped in your sin and rebellion, God chose you. By grace you are saved.

One thing is required of you: faith in Jesus. However, this faith goes beyond mere acknowledgment and mere words. It is a profound belief that should shape everything we do. It must follow the teachings and examples set in the Bible. Allow me to emphasize this point clearly. Just as those in the New Testament responded to Jesus with unwavering faith, I am determined to guide you in doing the same. With the utmost conviction, I affirm that the Bible is an inspired testament from God. Within its pages lies the roadmap to salvation, carefully revealed by God Himself. We should ground our beliefs in the truths found in the Bible. If God has instructed us to do something specific, I am committed to obeying.

The Road Ahead

Faith demands response.

When you believe that Jesus is the Son of God, everything changes—but the road doesn't end there. In fact, that's when the wheels really start turning. Real faith doesn't stand still. It moves. It speaks. It turns around. It surrenders. It obeys.

The Bible never separates belief from response. Faith is the engine, but it moves through action. Confession. Repentance. Baptism. Obedience. These aren't works that earn your salvation. They're mile markers that prove you're on the road.

In the next chapter, we'll trace that road. We'll look closely at how people responded when the gospel collided with their hearts for the first time. We'll step into the early church's story and see how real people, just like you, answered God's invitation to life.

Because faith that saves doesn't sit quietly.
It joins the journey.
And it walks the road all the way home.

The Circle of Faith

The Map That Makes Sense

*F*or it is by grace you have been saved, through faith —
*and this not from yourselves, it is the gift of God — not
by works, so that no one can boast. For we are God's workmanship, created in Christ Jesus to do good works, which God
prepared in advance for us to do.*

Several years ago, I had a map I used quite often. It was
called the DeLorme Atlas & Gazetteer: Tennessee. I probably still have it. The description on Amazon says "Exten-
sively indexed, full-color topographic maps provide infor-
mation on everything from cities and towns to historic
sites, scenic drives, trailheads, boat ramps, and even prime
fishing spots." I was interested in the "prime fishing spots"
part. I used it to find access points to rivers, streams,
and creeks where I could fish. It marked every interstate,
highway, gravel road, trail, and pig path. I would journey
out in adventure. I would take a small country road to a
little-known access point, trying to find a prime fishing spot.
It showed every tiny gravel stretch and creek-side path in
the state.

One day, I followed one of those little gray lines that wound
through a county I'd never explored. I wanted to check
out a potential fishing spot. The road started off paved,

then gravel, then dirt, then maybe path. (but that is a very generous description) The "road" kept getting smaller and smaller until my truck was bigger than the path. But, I kept going, trusting the map. But at the end of that so-called road, I didn't find a stream. I found a locked gate with a sign that read: Private Property. No Trespassing.

All I could do was sit there, truck idling, wondering how I was going to find a place to turn around. It wasn't the map's fault. I'm sure at one time that road went exactly where the map indicated. But things had changed. We often see it. A cool, old abandoned bridge that no longer carries traffic. A shell of a house in a patch of woods or in a field.

That fishing trip taught me something: Even good maps can feel wrong when the roads change. It wasn't that the map was broken. It was that something had shifted—quietly, over time. A new fence was built. A private gate put up. A road that used to be open had been claimed by someone else. And if you've ever tried to follow God's way in a world that keeps redrawing the lines, you know exactly how that feels.

Scripture gives us a map that leads plainly and clearly through confession, repentance, baptism, and a life of godliness. But over time, the spiritual landscape has shifted. Not because God changed—but because we did. Churches swapped surrender for comfort. Culture paved over obedience with opinion. And what used to be a clear path is now overgrown with religious detours and theological shortcuts.

But here's the truth: the original road still exists. The old path still leads home. And God's map still makes sense—if we're willing to follow it.

And faith—real faith—is a lot like that. Not every path that claims to lead to God actually does. Some roads are paved with good intentions, others with tradition or emotion or popular opinion. But Scripture gives us a map that makes sense. A path that's not just scenic, but saving.

In the New Testament, there are four landmarks that show up again and again on the route to life with God. You'll see them in Acts. In the epistles. On the lips of John the Baptist, Peter, Paul—even Jesus Himself.

Let's lay out the map.

Four particular landmarks forged one's faith in the New Testament. These four are consistent in Scripture. These four are prominent in conversion accounts in the New Testament, and all four are theologically important in New Testament passages. All four are of equal importance. One is not more important than the other.

I call them the Circle of Faith. What does faith look like? How do you tell if someone has faith? How does God view faith? If you are saved by grace through faith, for what type of faith response is God looking? The question must be answered within the context of what God says is important.

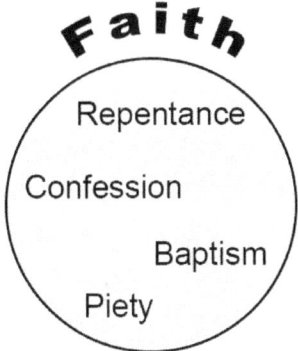

Here are the four faith responses in the New Testament: confession, repentance, baptism, and piety. There is no single conversion experience in the New Testament where all four are mentioned. Not one person is told to do all four things. If you are searching for examples to prove one more important than another, you won't have any problem. For example, Peter instructed people to repent in Acts 3, but he didn't mention confession. Paul was baptized, but repentance isn't mentioned. Acts 9 mentions that many people believed, but neither repentance, confession, nor baptism are mentioned.

You might ask, "If no one in Scripture is told to do all four—confession, repentance, baptism, piety—at the same time, are they really necessary?" Yes. Unequivocally, yes. But they're not pieces of a puzzle you put together one at a time. They're not boxes to check off like some kind of heavenly chore chart: confess—check. Repent—check. Get baptized—check. Live a godly life—check. That's not how the Spirit moves. That's not how surrender works.

We don't approach Jesus like we're planning a road trip. Imagine you are going to Las Vegas, and you want to see some other things while you are in the area. You look at a map and discover Hoover Dam, the Grand Canyon, and Zion National Park are relatively close. You map out a route: Las Vegas to Hoover Dam to the Grand Canyon to Zion National Park; then, back to Las Vegas. Conversion isn't a tour of spiritual landmarks—first confession, then repentance, on to baptism, then piety. That kind of journey has a planned sequence, a carefully plotted route. Conversion isn't like that.

Conversion is a collision. Not a chronology.

It's the moment when the gospel crashes into your heart. It's a breaking and a mending all at once. It's when the truth of Jesus doesn't just whisper—it thunders. And when that thunder rolls through your soul, confession, repentance, baptism, and piety don't happen in neat, separated stages. They erupt like a volcano. They spill out together like a dam breaking. It's all one moment. One surrender. One cry of, "What must I do?" met with one life-changing answer: "Come to Jesus."

We aren't approaching these as a checklist to be done in a specific order. They aren't four different destinations. They are simultaneous, not sequential. The order or timing isn't of chief importance. Your response to Jesus is of chief importance.

The order isn't the point. The heart is.

The formula isn't the power. Jesus is.

If your soul is convicted but not confessing, something's missing.

If your life turns from sin but never turns toward God, something's missing.

If you believe but haven't died and risen with Him in baptism, something's missing.

If your faith has no fruit, no fire, no pursuit of holiness, something's missing.

We don't need to get stuck trying to diagram the journey. Conversion isn't like steps on a staircase. Conversion is like the rush of a river, all at once.

So don't worry about the sequence. Worry about the Savior. Look at Him. Listen to Him. And let your life shout, "Yes."

These four landmarks are also not meritorious works. A meritorious work is a work which obligates God to do something because you did something. It's another way of saying we earn salvation. Let's be clear. We do not earn salvation. All discussion must center on the person and work of Jesus. Salvation begins and ends with God's grace. No action obligates God to save you. These aren't things you do to earn salvation. They are the key responses and indicators of faith.

What is considered a work? Typically, we define a work as something a human being does. How does that connect with spiritual thought? First, there is some truth in that. We confess. We repent. We are baptized. We live godly lives. We perform and engage in those actions. When Paul writes something like *not by works, so that no one can boast*, he doesn't mean that humans don't do anything. He means that nothing humans do obligates God to save.

Confession, repentance, baptism, and piety aren't hoops we jump through to earn God's favor. They're the response of a heart that's already been gripped by His grace. These aren't transactions. They're transformations. Confession isn't payment—it's surrender. Repentance isn't a ritual—it's a turning away from what kills us. Baptism isn't a badge—it's burial and rebirth, a divine act clothed in water. Piety isn't performance—it's presence. These are not human achievements that obligate God to act. Salvation isn't wage-earned. It is a gift extended by the grace and mercy of God. These steps don't earn grace. They reveal it. They are a response to God's grace.

We will look at the faith responses to the gospel through two lenses. The first will be groups. The second will consist of individuals. You will notice some key differences in detail between them.

The Crowd Believed—But That Wasn't All

If we study the responses of groups to the message of Jesus, we find the most frequent description of the conversion experience is belief. The book of Acts provides the most examples of how people responded to the gospel. The epistles explain more theological truths concerning the four landmarks, but each will be explored in its own chapter.

When the gospel swept through the streets of Jerusalem, the hills of Judea, the markets of Philippi, and the synagogues of Corinth, it didn't just move individuals—it shook entire crowds, households, cities, and regions. The message of Jesus didn't whisper into one ear at a time. It thundered through communities. And people responded.

Across the book of Acts, we find seventeen different moments where **groups** of people heard the gospel and made a choice. You can see them in this chart.

Group	Believe	Repentance	Confession	Baptism
Acts 2:37-38				
Acts 3:19				
Acts 4:4				
Acts 5:14				
Acts 6:7				
Acts 8:12				
Acts 9:35				
Acts 9:42				
Acts 10:47				
Acts 11:21				
Acts 13:48				
Acts 14:1				
Acts 17:12				
Acts 18:7-8				
Acts 19:1-7				
Acts 19:18				
Acts 26:19-20				

In twelve of those, the word used is **belief**. The crowd believed. Many believed. A great number of Jews and Greeks believed. Again and again, belief described the response to the gospel.

But it's not the only one.

Five of those group responses mention **baptism**. It wasn't reserved for the few or the brave or the spiritual elite. Baptism happened in cities, groups, and households. Baptism was public and immediate. There was no hesitation.

Five mention **repentance**. That means turning—changing direction. Whole communities left old lives, old loyalties, and old gods. They didn't just add Jesus to their shelf. They cleared the shelf.

Only one mentions **confession**—but it's there. And it matters. Because in the early church, silence wasn't an option. Sins were openly confessed and acknowledged. The name of Jesus was publicly declared.

Now here's what is easy to miss.

If we just counted words, we'd think belief was all that mattered. It's mentioned the most. It's the simplest to say. But Scripture doesn't count like we do. It invites us to trace the pattern. And the pattern is always movement. Belief was just the ignition. Baptism, repentance, confession, piety — those were the gears that got the wheels turning.

The reason belief shows up the most in group responses is because it's the gateway. The starting point. But in Acts, belief that stands alone never stands for long. The crowds that truly believed confessed their sins and the name of Jesus. They were baptized. They turned from sin. They lived differently.

Faith started in their hearts, but it consumed every part of their being.

When the gospel came, it called for more than agreement. It called for surrender. And the faithful didn't just believe. They followed.

When It Got Personal, They Got Committed

The gospel wasn't just for crowds. It reached the one sitting in a chariot. The one guarding a prison. The one praying by a river. The one watching from the shadows. It didn't just stir cities—it stopped individuals in their tracks.

Eight times in the book of Acts, we see a single person come face to face with the message of Jesus. Each one unique. A sorcerer. A eunuch. A tentmaker. A soldier. A jailer. A merchant. A governor. A persecutor-turned-apostle.

Person	Believe	Repentance	Confession	Baptism
Simon (Acts 8)				
Eunuch (Acts 8)			?	
Paul (Acts 9)				
Cornelius (Acts 10)				
Sergius Paulus (Acts 13)				
Lydia (Acts 16)				
Jailer (Acts 16)				
Crispus (Acts 18)				

Four of those stories mention **belief**. That moment when the light breaks in. When a heart says yes. When a man or woman realizes Jesus isn't just real—He's Lord.

But belief wasn't the only word.

Six of those eight stories mention **baptism**. That's no co-incidence. When it got personal, people didn't wait. They didn't schedule it weeks out. They didn't overthink it. They got in the water. They buried the old life and came up new. The eunuch begged to be baptized on the spot. Paul was baptized three days after being blinded by glory. The jailer and his family were baptized in the middle of the night, right after washing the apostles' wounds.

The Ethiopian eunuch might hint at confession. The original text probably didn't include the verses on confessing the name of Jesus. Most newer translations correctly reference the later reading in a footnote. Because of that, a question mark was placed in the chart.

But here's what catches most by surprise. None of the individual stories use the word repentance.

That doesn't mean they didn't repent. It means the repentance showed up in action. In obedience. In urgency. Simon the Sorcerer is rebuked for false motives—his life didn't match the move. But for the rest, repentance wasn't just spoken. It was lived. Paul left behind persecution and picked up preaching. The jailer left fear behind and stepped into hospitality and healing. Lydia opened her home. Cornelius gathered his whole household to listen to Peter.

Their lives turned. Their fruit proved it.

When faith got personal, it got costly. But it also got real. They didn't wait for the next revival or a perfect moment. They believed. They obeyed. The proclaimed the lordship of Jesus. They changed their lives. They got in the water. They lived their faith.

Because when the gospel meets a willing heart, the only question left is: "What are you waiting for?"

Conclusion: The Circle Isn't Broken—But It Must Be Complete

Again, no single person in Acts was told to do all five things. You won't find one verse that says, "Believe, confess, repent, be baptized, and walk in godliness." But you will find all five—over and over—woven through every story where someone truly turned to Jesus. Some were told to believe. Some were told to repent. Some were told to be baptized. Some confessed. Some were commended for godly living.

The circle isn't laid out as a checklist—it is lived out as a rhythm. A pattern. A pulse. And when you trace the footsteps of the faithful, you'll find every landmark in place.

Belief was the spark.
Confession was the voice.
Repentance was the turn.
Baptism was the burial and birth.
Godliness was the new road they walked.

Take one away, and something vital is missing. Pull one out, and the shape doesn't hold. Each piece matters. Every one of them is a response to grace. Every one is a call from the cross. Not one of them earns salvation. But together, they show what saving faith really does.

It believes.
It confesses.
It turns.
It surrenders.
It walks.

Don't settle for one spoke on the wheel. Don't stop halfway around the circle. The gospel didn't come to spark a moment—it came to launch a movement. One that begins in the heart and drives through every part of your life.

God still draws maps. The road is still marked. The landmarks haven't moved.

The circle is waiting. Stomp the gas.

The Road Ahead

The gospel invites a response—and now the road begins to narrow.

You've seen how the early church responded when the good news shattered their old way of life. They didn't just believe in their hearts. They acted. They repented. They were baptized. They began to walk in obedience. The circle of faith was never abstract. It was public. Embodied. Lived.

Confession is more than reciting a line. It's a surrender of allegiance. A clear, unwavering cry: *Jesus is Lord.* Those words cost early Christians everything—family, comfort, safety, even life. But they said them anyway. Because once you believe, you speak. Once you see the truth, you name it.

In the next chapter, we'll step into the gravity of that confession. We'll explore what it means to declare Jesus not just as Savior, but as King. Not just with our lips, but with our lives.

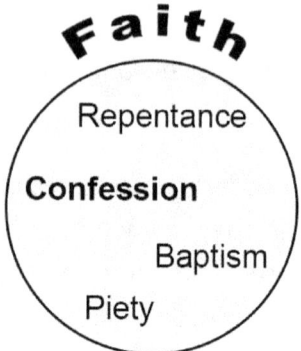

Confession

Owning the Wrong Turn

I believe Jesus is the Son of God. The words are simple. No syllables to stumble over. No hidden meanings to decode. Yet that single statement carries more weight than any other sentence you will ever speak. Its implications stretch beyond time and history. It is an eternal confession. When the world as we know it passes away, that truth will remain. *Jesus Christ is the same yesterday, today, and forever.* (Hebrews 13:8) He existed before creation's first breath, and He will reign long after the last breath of this world. And Jesus Christ—the eternal, unchanging Son of God—is the One who will grant you everlasting life because of your confession.

Truth in a World That Calls You Foolish

But confessing Jesus as Christ is not easy. Not in a world like this. Many in our world view Christians as old-fashioned, out-of-touch, narrow-minded, bigoted, foolish, unreasonable, intolerant, incompetent, even dangerous. They claim we've been left behind, unable to keep up with what they call "truth." They pride themselves on being more enlightened, more evolved than the simple teachings of Jesus. These worldviews aren't merely different. They are at war with each other. There's no middle ground. No compromise between the wisdom of God and the thinking of man. As Scripture says, *A natural man does not accept the things of the Spirit of God, for they are foolishness to him; and he cannot understand them, because they are spiritually discerned.* (1 Corinthians 2:14)

Pilate once stood face to face with Jesus and asked, *What is truth?* (John 18:38) He asked the question, but he couldn't hear the answer. The answer had already been spoken. Jesus had just declared, *For this reason I was born, and for this I came into the world in order that I might testify to the truth. Everyone who is of the truth listens to My voice.* (John 18:37) Jesus didn't point Pilate to a system or a theory. He pointed him to Himself. Earlier in His ministry, He had already made it plain: *I am the way, the truth, and the life.* (John 14:6)

Confession is an Anchor

Truth isn't altered by time or opinion. It isn't reshaped by culture or softened by pressure. The truth of Jesus stands, unchanging and eternal. To confess Jesus is to align your life with unshakable truth. It is to stand firm when everything else is shifting. It is to say with clarity and conviction: "This is where I stand, and this is Who I follow."

Confession is more than a statement of belief. It is a declaration of allegiance. And that allegiance will anchor your soul — and offend the world.

Confession isn't for the faint-hearted. It takes courage to say the words, and even more courage to live them out. To confess Jesus as the Christ is not a one-time event. It's a daily decision. A choice to walk in the truth when it costs you something. A choice to stay faithful when the pressure mounts. A choice to say with your life what your lips declare. Jesus never promised it would be easy. *Whoever confesses me before men, I will confess before my Father in heaven. But whoever denies me before men, I will deny him before my Father in heaven.* (Matthew 10:32–33)

Consequences of Confession

That is not a verse to breeze past. Jesus draws a line in eternity, and the stakes are eternal. Jesus makes it plain — your confession matters. Confession is not just about speaking truth. It's about standing in it, no matter the cost. It's not just about professing belief. It's about proving loyalty. To confess Jesus is to align yourself with Him in public and in private. It is to name Him as Lord in front of others — and to keep Him as Lord when no one is watching. Confession is not an accessory to faith. Confession is a matter of spiritual survival.

Confession is a public declaration. It confirms your belief that Jesus is the Son of God. It declares your allegiance to Him as Lord. It acknowledges your conviction that Jesus is the Messiah, the Savior of the world. Confession is a lifestyle, not an event. Confession is not meant to be hidden in a private memory. It is meant to be carried into public obedience. Those who believe that Jesus is the Son of God must confess Him with both word and life. Confessing

Jesus is a daily action which shapes every decision, thought, and relationship.

If Jesus is Lord, you must understand a simple truth. If Jesus is Lord, you are not! That is a simple, but profound, life-altering statement. That statement is simple, but it will change your life. It removes pride. It shatters self-centeredness. It confronts the illusion that we belong to ourselves. The world says, "It's my life." Jesus says, *You are not your own; you were bought at a price.* (1 Corinthians 6:19–20) To confess Jesus as Lord admits you belong to Him. Your plans, your time, your heart — every part of you belongs to Him. Confession doesn't just change your eternity. It reorders your present.

You are so much more than a random, short-term collection of decisions, circumstances, and events. You are more than a brief flash of years followed by silence. You are not a cosmic accident or a product of random events. You are God's masterpiece. He formed you with care. He shaped you with purpose. He placed His image in you and called you His own. Any fulfillment you find outside of God's design will always run dry. It may last for a season. It may feel satisfying for a time. But it will not endure. You might experience eighty or a hundred years of self-fulfillment. But what about the millions of years after that? What about the eternity still to come? Eternal purpose can only be found in the Lordship of Jesus Christ.

Notice what's at stake. I didn't say you may or may not have eternal life. You will. Everyone will. The only question is where. The only question is whether your eternity will be filled with life or loss, joy or judgment, presence or sep-aration. You are a work of art—one-of-a-kind, intention-ally handcrafted by divine genius. Don't waste the design. Embrace it. Let the life He gave you become the life that honors Him.

Wholeheartedly acknowledge Jesus as the divine Son of God! Acknowledge Him as the supreme Ruler above all rulers, and the highest Authority among all authorities. This profound declaration has the power to transform and redefine your entire life.

Confession requires honesty. If Jesus is Lord, everything in your life must come under His authority. That doesn't just mean your words. It means your motives and choices. What are some areas of your life challenged by the Lord-ship of Jesus? Where are you still trying to stay in control?

For example, it is easy to say God is more important than money. Our relationship with finances must be important because finances triggered one of Jesus' strongest warn-ings. *A man cannot serve two masters. Either he will hate the one and love the other, or he will be devoted to the one and despise the other. You cannot serve both God and money.* (Matthew 6:24) It sounds easy to say "all of my money belongs to God. He can have it all." It takes real honesty to determine if that is true. There are signs. Are you generous? Or are you stingy? Are you sacrificial in your giving? Do you give regularly and consistently to God? How does your contribution compare to other expenditures? Do you give to God first, or only after you have spent on yourself? If you don't give to God but spend extravagantly on yourself, you need to examine your priorities.

I remember a moment in class when someone asked whether they should base their giving on pre-tax or after-tax income. Another member spoke up and said, "Well, do you want God to bless you pre-tax or post-tax?" It was a lighthearted answer, but it made a serious point.

This isn't a chapter about money. It's about confession. Confession requires that Jesus is Lord of all. Money just happens to be one of the clearest places where Lordship gets tested. Money pulls at the heart. Money promises security. Money whispers self-reliance. It's one thing to say, "God owns it all." It's another thing to live like He does.

The validity of the principle extends to every part of your life. Does Jesus have control of your relationships? Do you have a relationship pulling you toward compromise? Do you have a relationship with a friend that sways you to ungodly behavior? Are you in a dating relationship that isn't honoring God — emotionally, physically, or spiritually? It could be a relationship with a spouse, a parent, a child, or a sibling. A relationship in which you know the choices you are making aren't spiritually healthy, but you are afraid to make a godly decision. Or a relationship in which you find self-worth instead of letting Jesus provide your self-worth. That doesn't mean we avoid every relationship with those who lack the faith to confess the lordship of Jesus. We are called to help others find faith in Jesus. Jesus sends us into the world to be salt and light. However, we must honestly evaluate those relationships that are toxic to our faith.

There is a difference between being shaped by others and God helping you shape others. Some relationships help you confess Jesus as Lord. Some cause us to forget that Jesus is Lord. Confession must reach into your relationships. If Jesus is Lord, the people in your life must not take His place.

Is Jesus Lord of your career? That question reaches deeper than where you work. It reaches into why you work. It asks what you're chasing. It examines what you are willing to sacrifice. It cross-examines what you're willing to do to get ahead—and what you're willing to surrender to stay faithful. It's easy to separate your spiritual life from your professional life. It's tempting to clock in and leave your convictions at the door. Often we tell ourselves or we hear from others: It's just business. But confession doesn't work like that. If Jesus is Lord, then He's Lord in the boardroom. He is Lord on the job site and Lord in every office, meeting, and decision. He's not just Lord on Sunday morning. He's Lord on Monday morning. That doesn't mean you have to quit your job and only work in ministry. It means the way you work should reflect to whom you belong. Your integrity. Your humility. Your purpose. Your priorities. Are you honest when honesty costs you something? Are you kind when no one notices? Are you willing to say no to success if success means denying Christ? Confession isn't something you leave at church. It goes with you to work.

Is Jesus Lord of your entertainment choices? That question isn't just about what you watch. It's about what you welcome. It's about what you invite into your heart and your mind. Not everything you enjoy is harmless. Not

everything that makes you laugh is healthy. Not everything that entertains you honors Christ. We live in a world
overflowing with content — television, movies, music, social media, podcasts, video games. We stream it, scroll it,
and repeat it—often without thinking. But the things we
consume shape the people we become. They train our
thoughts. They harden our hearts. They stir up desires
we were meant to crucify. You can't confess Jesus as Lord
and continually feed on things that mock His name. You
can't ask Him to guard your heart while giving the world
unrestricted access to your soul. Confession must reach
into your habits. What entertains you eventually influences
you. And what influences you will shape who you become.

Confession Creates a Sounding Board

Confession creates a sounding board for priorities. By consistently acknowledging Jesus as our Lord, we compel ourselves to scrutinize how our desires, priorities, and plans
align with this declaration. It reveals what matters most. It
exposes where our loyalties lie. It challenges how our plans
align with God's purpose. Confession becomes a lens that
invites Christ's authority to look into every area of our lives.
It challenges how our plans align with God's purpose. The
Lordship of Jesus demands a simple, powerful statement:
Let your will be done.

Jesus prayed in agony to the Father in Gethsemane. *My
Father, if it is possible, may this cup be taken from me. Yet,
not as I will, but as You will.* (Matthew 26:39) He didn't want
the pain, but He chose obedience. He didn't shrink from

difficulty. He didn't retreat from surrender. That's what confession looks like.

We must make the same confession: "Jesus, whatever you desire for me in this life, let your will be done." If Jesus is the Son of God, Jesus is Lord. If Jesus is Lord, Jesus must control your life.

Confession of Jesus' lordship becomes visible in our prayers. When Jesus taught His disciples to pray, Jesus included this petition. *Let Your will be done on earth as it is in heaven.* (Matthew 6:10) That isn't a soft request. It is a confession. God's will must take precedence over our desires. It means surrender isn't optional. Surrender is foundational.

What do your prayers reflect? Do your prayers reflect God's desires or just your own? Do they seek His direction or seek His approval for plans you've already made? Do they confess His lordship or attempt to negotiate His will?

The goal of spiritual maturity is not to silence your desires. It is to reshape them. Spiritual maturity leads to a place where what you want and what God wants are the same. So start every day with confession. Say it out loud. Say it in your heart. Say it until it becomes the filter for every decision you make.

Jesus, I believe you are the Christ, the Son of God. Jesus, help me pledge my allegiance to You. Jesus, I'm struggling with . . . How does that fit into Your plans?

Confession reorients our hearts. It reminds us that we are not Lord. That's not a loss. That is a gift.

Confession Seals

I have a Ford F-150 I bought new in 1992. That truck is an extension of me. I'll probably own it my entire life. Or, at least if I have my way, I will. I've had it longer than my sons. I drove the boys to school in that old truck. It's the 2nd favorite vehicle I have owned (just behind the '67 Mustang). Years ago, it started leaking oil — not just from one place, from several places. The oil pan gasket, the valve cover gasket, and the push-rod cover gasket were all leaking. The purpose of the gasket is to keep oil from leaking out. If the gasket is worn or broken, oil leaks out of the engine. You might smell it burning on the engine. You might see oil on the driveway. When you see or smell those signs, you know something is off. Confession is like that. It's a spiritual gasket that seals the heart.

We also had to replace a seal on the back door. The purpose of that seal was just as important. That seal kept warm air in and cold air out in the winter. Or cold air in and warm air out in the summer. When the seal leaks, air escapes. Temperature shifts. Comfort disappears.

In a similar fashion, confession seals our hearts. Confession keeps the good things in and the bad things out. When we constantly test our actions against the lordship of Christ, the discrepancies become obvious. We see the "oil leaks." We feel the cold air slipping out of the house. We notice the draft escaping from our soul.

Christians face the challenge of maintaining a pure heart in a world inundated with ungodly influences. We are constantly bombarded by the ungodly influences of people, television, radio, internet, music, and social platforms. While these things aren't inherently bad, they can be evil influences if they aren't filtered. It can be difficult to block these things and keep our hearts focused on God. Satan entered the heart of Judas, and Satan wants to enter your heart. Satan wants to confuse you. He wants to rearrange your priorities. He wants to pull your focus toward the wrong things. He wants to make sure that eternal things, spiritual things, and godly things are pushed to the back of your mind. Satan wants you focused on worldly, temporary things. Remember our analogy of the truck? If the oil leaks out of the engine, the engine will be destroyed. If we don't notice the leak, we might not even realize it's happening. Confession helps us notice the leaks caused by Satan's deception. Confession brings the problem to light—so we can take the steps to make it right.

Confession seals our hearts. If you confess "I believe Jesus is the Son of God," that confession will keep your heart focused. Your heart follows your treasure. That's what Jesus said. *Where your treasure is, there your heart will be also.* (Matthew 6:21) When you regularly confess the Lordship of Christ, you remind yourself where your treasure truly lies. You re-center your affections. You re-align your direction. That is why it is crucial to engage in daily confession.

Say it when you wake up. Say it before the meeting. Say it when the pressure builds. Say it when you're tempted. Say it when you're uncertain. Say it even when you're struggling to believe it. Confession is not just for the moment of salvation. It's for the fight to stay faithful.

We don't realize the power of self-talk. Self-talk is the voice in your head. The quiet commentary that questions, criticizes, and second-guesses.

During my time in sales, I would occasionally find myself circling the block, gathering the courage to make a new sales call. It wasn't the actual call that posed a problem, but rather the internal dialogue in my head. I was plagued by questions like, "What if I face rejection?" or "What if they refuse to see me?" or "What if I embarrass myself?" These negative thoughts convinced me that humiliation and rejection were inevitable. In reality, the sales calls were rarely unpleasant experiences. I faced rejection often. Instances of mistreatment were rare. No one ever assaulted me. Most people were just busy, yet generally pleasant. Overcoming the self-doubt that resided in my mind proved to be quite challenging. Negative self-talk has the power to immobilize our actions, while positive self-talk empowers us to embrace new experiences and take risks.

Satan knows how to use those negative voices. He doesn't have to attack us from the outside if he can get in our heads. He tells you that you aren't good enough. He tries to convince you that you've failed too many times. He wants us to believe God could never love us. Satan deceives you into thinking God would never forgive your sins. He tricks you into thinking God would never rescue you and bring you into His glorious, wonderful kingdom. If Satan can convince us through self-doubt that we are never good enough for God, we will never make the public confession of Jesus Christ. We will always feel like we just aren't the kind of person Jesus wants. We will always feel like we can't accomplish the things that God intends for us.

When we confess the Lordship of Jesus Christ, we redirect those voices in our heads back to a spiritual core. We silence the voice of shame with grace. We push out fear by proclaiming faith. We expose insecurity by declaring identity. If Jesus Christ is Lord of lords and King of kings, then Jesus Christ can rescue me from my sin. Since Jesus went to the cross for my sin, then no voice can unwrite what He has written. Feeling unworthy can actually deepen our faith. Instead of being consumed by self-doubt, we choose to trust the voice that speaks mercy over us. Inadequacy reminds us we were never meant to save ourselves. It drives us to the One who can.

Confession helps us recognize our imperfections and surrender them to God. It allows us to find security in His grace, understanding that it was our very imperfections that prompted God to send His Son to redeem us. Through confessing our sins, we acknowledge our own unworthiness and brokenness. We come to realize that we are not flawless, perfect beings; we are flawed, imperfect beings. And Jesus came to save unworthy, broken, imperfect people. Jesus came to save us.

The act of confessing our sins presents us with a chance to embrace the power of forgiveness. Confessing our sin allows us to acknowledge our sinfulness in a healthy way. Confession helps us acknowledge our unworthiness and brokenness. We come to terms with what we are—not flawless, but flawed. Not perfect, but deeply in need of grace.

Confession removes secrecy and insecurity. When we confess the Lordship of Jesus vocally, something changes. Our out-loud statement contrasts our inner doubt. That why praying out loud produces a different dynamic than praying in our heads. Expressing something vocally is different than thinking about something. Vocal confession peels back the layers of secrecy in our hearts. It also helps overcome insecurity. When we vocalize something, it helps confirm our conviction. If you say it more, you will believe it more. If you proclaim it, you will be more secure in its truth. This isn't some mind game. God will strengthen and confirm your confession by His Spirit which He gave to guide, encourage, and convict you.

What prevents us from confessing Jesus as Lord?

Roadblocks of Confession

For many, it's fear. Sometimes that fear is loud—like rejection, ridicule, or exclusion. Sometimes it's quieter—like hesitation, discomfort, or the worry that someone might think differently of us. But fear—loud or soft—can silence faith.

In John 9, Jesus healed a man who was born blind. The miracle should've been cause for celebration. But when the Pharisees started asking questions, the man's parents froze. They passed the responsibility back to their son. John records, *His parents said this because they were afraid of the Jews, for already the Jews had decided that anyone who confessed Jesus as Christ would be put out of the synagogue.* (John 9:22)

The parents were afraid of the consequences of openly acknowledging Jesus as the Messiah. The Jewish leaders had already decreed that anyone who confessed faith in Jesus would be expelled from the synagogue. Their fear stemmed from their apprehension toward the religious authorities and the possibility of being rejected. Instead of experiencing pure joy and gratitude for their son's miraculous healing, they found themselves weighed down by anxiety and uncertainty.

Later in John's gospel, some of the Jewish leaders believed. *Yet at the same time many even among the leaders believed in him. But because of the Pharisees they would not confess their faith for fear they would be put out of the synagogue; for they loved praise from men more than praise from God.* (John 12:42-43) They were convinced. But instead of proclaiming faith in Jesus, they remained silent. It reminds me of Jesus' words. *Whoever confesses me before men, I will confess before my Father in heaven. Whoever denies me before men, I will deny him before my Father in heaven.* (Matthew 10:32-33)

We can love the praise of men more than praise from God. When we are afraid to acknowledge our faith in Jesus because we are afraid of what others might think of us, we love the praise of men more than the praise of God. When we refuse to acknowledge our faith in Jesus because we think others might exclude us, we love the praise of men more than the praise of God. When we don't acknowledge our faith in Jesus because we are afraid others might make fun of us or ridicule us, we love the praise of men more than the praise of God. When we are afraid or refuse, in any circumstance, to confess Jesus as the Son of God, we are in danger of Jesus denying His relationship with us. If we deny Him, He will deny us.

The world will not understand us. The world will exclude us. The world will persecute us. The world will hate us. It hated Jesus first. And Jesus said it would hate us too. The message of Revelation anchors our souls. Jesus is the conqueror. He rides on a white horse, faithful and true. Jesus will conquer every plan of Satan. Satan's defeat has already been sealed by the cross. Jesus said, *Do not be afraid of what you are about to suffer. I tell you, the devil will put some of you in prison to test you, and you will suffer persecution for ten days. Be faithful, even to the point of death, and I will give you the crown of life.* (Revelation 2:10)

That is the call of confession. To stay faithful when it costs you something. To speak His name when silence would be safer. To stand with Jesus when the world walks away.

So set your mind free from the fear of this world. The world can kill the body, but not the soul. It can end your life, but not your existence. Your confession of Jesus is eternal. Don't let temporary pain steal eternal joy. Confess the lordship of Jesus.

We don't just confess in our own minds and by our lifestyle. We confess before the church. We profess Jesus as the Son of God—not just in private belief, but in public allegiance. If we can't say His name among believers, we won't say it when the pressure builds. If we stay silent in a place of safety, we'll crumble in a place of hostility. Public confession isn't a ritual. It's not a script. It's not an incantation of magical words. It's a declaration: "Jesus is Lord, and I trust Him with everything I am." In that moment, we draw a line in the sand. We place our hope in Christ. We make a stand.

That's not the end. That's the beginning. Because confession starts a journey—one that stretches into every crevice of your life.

But confession is not just a statement. It's a lifestyle. To confess Jesus as the Son of God means you honor Him in every area of your life—your job, your family, your money, your friendships, your habits, your hobbies. There is no corner of your life where the Lordship of Jesus doesn't matter. If Jesus is Lord, then you are not. That truth changes everything.

Confession isn't where the journey ends—it's where transformation begins.

So let me ask you plainly:
Will you stand before your church and say it out loud?
Will you name Jesus in front of those who already love Him—and then go declare Him to a world that doesn't?
Will you speak His name without shame?
Will you proclaim what you believe—not just with your mouth, but with your whole life?

I believe Jesus is the Son of God.
Are you ready to say it?

The Road Ahead

Confession is where the truth comes out. Repentance is where the change begins.

You've said the words. You've made the claim. Jesus is Lord. But that declaration demands more than breath—it demands a break. A break from sin. A break from old patterns. A break from self.

Confession says, "I believe."
Repentance says, "I will change."

Not change by willpower. Not change for appearances. But a deep, Spirit-driven turning—a transformation that reaches all the way down to the root.

In the next chapter, we'll step into that holy turn. We'll talk about what repentance really means, and why it matters so much to God. Because the narrow road doesn't just ask, "Who do you say I am?" It asks, "Will you leave everything behind to follow Me?"

Let's take that step together. Let's talk about repentance.

Repentance
Making the U-Turn

For by grace you are saved through faith. And this is not your own doing; it is the gift of God, not a result of works, so that no one may boast. For we are His workmanship, created in Christ Jesus for good works, which God prepared ahead of time, that we should walk in them. (Ephesians 2:8–10)

On December 10, 2021, I wasn't watching the sky. I was sitting at my desk reviewing the church's livestream data when a video feed from a television station in Arkansas caught my attention. They were tracking a tornado—massive, steady, and unlike anything they had seen before. The weatherman's voice broke as he spoke. "I've never seen anything like this." "The debris field rises to 50,000 feet."

I quickly located the station's livestream and began watching. I couldn't look away. The tornado was marching across northeast Arkansas, refusing to weaken. It wasn't wobbling or fading. It was gaining strength, and it was headed toward the Bootheel of Missouri. That meant one thing. If it kept its path, it would strike Hornbeak. That's where my parents lived.

I grabbed the phone and called. "Are you watching the weather?" I asked. "There's a massive tornado headed your way."

In the house where I grew up, we had what we called a safe spot—a small closet under the stairs in the back bedroom. I'm not sure how much safety it could really offer, but it was the best option we had. It was at the center of the house, away from windows and outside walls. They told me they were already in the closet. I'm not sure they were. Most likely, they didn't want me to worry.

Tornadoes are not something to play with. They demand respect. They do not wait for you to prepare. You take them seriously, and you act quickly.

I started watching two television stations. One in Memphis and one in Paducah. I tracked the storm as it crossed the Mississippi River into Tennessee. My concern turned to alarm. A tornado of that strength would obliterate Hornbeak if it didn't change course.

Just after crossing the Mississippi River, the tornado veered north. Hornbeak was spared. Reelfoot Lake and Samburg were not. The storm struck them with unrelenting force.

Somewhere over western Obion County—northeast of Samburg—the tornado dissipated. That's how storms like that end. One moment, the sky is full of fury. The next, it's gone. The danger disappears, but the fear it leaves behind takes longer to settle.

Almost immediately, another tornado formed near Woodland Mills. This one continued north, carving a trail of destruction through Mayfield and across western Kentucky. At first, we believed it was one single, unbroken tornado stretching across four states. Only later would we learn the truth: five separate tornadoes, each with its own path of devastation.

But in that moment, I wasn't thinking about meteorology. I was thinking about my parents. And I wanted one thing: immediate action.

I had called long before the tornado reached the Mississippi River. I wasn't interested in panic or fear—I simply wanted them in the safest place they could find. I wanted them to move before the danger became visible.

Because when you're given new knowledge—especially the kind that could change everything—you don't just sit there. You act.

In this case, the new knowledge was simple: a massive tornado was heading straight for Mom and Dad. That changed my entire perspective. I wasn't waiting for more data. I wasn't interested in probabilities. I didn't want them passing GO and collecting $200, as the Monopoly card says. I wanted them in that closet—now! I wanted action! I wanted behavior to change based on what we now knew. A storm like that doesn't give you time to weigh your options. A tornado heading your way demands one thing: get to safety before it's too late.

Repentance originates from faith. It begins with a change of mind that produces a change of behavior. Yet too often, we focus on behavior and miss the deeper issue. Real repentance does not start with trying harder. It starts with seeing clearer. Behavior will never consistently change without a change of mind.

When we truly understand and embrace the truth that Jesus is the Son of God who became flesh to redeem our sins, our entire perspective shifts. Everything about how we see the world, ourselves, and our purpose changes. That change of mind becomes a spiritual catalyst. It permeates every fiber of our being. It burns through our excuses. It reorders our desires.

When you believe that Jesus is the Son of God, you realize that everything was created for His glory: you, others, nature, the universe, your family, your career, your hobbies, your possessions, and your passions. Everything revolves around the person of Jesus Christ. We simply cannot be the same after we believe in Jesus. His Lordship shakes the core of our existence.

Faith in Jesus demands radical repentance. It is not enough to have a fleeting thought of becoming more godly or casually turning away from sin. Radical repentance requires a genuine, whole-hearted commitment to eradicate the cancer of sin from our lives and pursue godliness.

It's not easy to change behavior. Especially when the behavior has been part of you for years. If it were easy to quit doing things detrimental to our spiritual health, everyone would do it. It's hard to break old habits and form new ones. Deep patterns don't disappear with good intentions. They must be surrendered to God, fought with grace, and replaced by something better.

Sin digs deep. It rewires our reactions. It comforts us, even as it kills us. And repentance calls us to walk away from it—not just once, but over and over again. It's not a moment of guilt. It's a lifelong movement of surrender. Real repentance isn't surface-level. It isn't just behavior modification. You might be able to fake obedience for a while, but you won't be able to sustain it without a transformed heart.

Repentance is anchored in the heart, not in willpower. We cannot consistently change behavior without changing our hearts. It is not an external act but a fundamental shift in our inner being. True repentance demands a genuine change of heart where our motives, desires, and convictions are transformed. Only through this transformation can we consistently alter our behavior and break free from the shackles of our past actions. Without transformation of the heart, any attempt to change our behavior will only be temporary and superficial. Repentance changes how we think, not just how we act. It is a total change of thought and behavior. Lasting change starts from within, at the very core of our being.

John the Baptist didn't step out of the wilderness with a whisper. He came roaring like a prophet of old—wild, bold, unapologetic. His voice cracked through the dry silence of a spiritually dead generation. His message was simple, but it shook the crowds to their core.

Repent, for the kingdom of heaven is near. (Matthew 3:2)

He wasn't talking to pagans or idol worshipers. He was talking to religious people—people who thought they were safe, people who thought repentance was for someone else. John made it clear. If you think belonging to Abraham is enough, you're in trouble. If you think God's kingdom will be satisfied with empty rituals, you're mistaken. If you want to be ready for the Messiah, it's time to change.

John's message demanded action. The crowds heard him, and they didn't argue theology. They asked the only question that matters when repentance is real: "What should we do?" John didn't give a deep theological treatise. The one with two coats should share with the person who doesn't have one. The person with food should share with the one who is hungry. Soldiers, those in positions of authority, shouldn't intimidate others. Tax collectors, those in financial control, shouldn't take advantage of others.

John's words were a warning—but also an invitation. God was drawing near. The Messiah was coming. And the only right response was radical, visible, obedient change.

John wanted people to take action. John wanted people to change because the reality had changed. The kingdom of heaven, the kingdom of God, was entering the world in a new way.

John the Baptist preached repentance. He demanded fruit. He called for visible change. But even as the people responded, the question still lingered in the shadows: How do you sustain that kind of change? Where does the power come from to keep turning away from sin—not just once, but again and again?

That's where Romans 8 speaks. *Those who live according to the flesh have their minds set on what the flesh desires; but those who live in accordance with the Spirit have their minds set on what the Spirit desires. The mind set on the flesh is death, but the mind controlled by the Spirit is life and peace; the mind set on the flesh is hostile to God. It does not submit to God's law, nor can it do so. Those controlled by the flesh cannot please God.* (Romans 8:5-8)

Paul describes two kinds of people: those who live according to the flesh, and those who live according to the Spirit. These are not just different behaviors—they are different worlds. Two roads. Two mindsets. Two destinies.

The flesh resists God. It refuses to surrender. It clings to control, comfort, and compromise. It doesn't care about fruit—it only craves survival.

When your mind is governed by the flesh—by your old patterns, your old instincts, your old self—you're headed toward death. No matter how sincere your intentions, the flesh will always pull you back into what you were. It will rationalize sin. It will fight surrender. It will whisper, "You're fine. Don't change. You can't change."

But when the Spirit enters your life, everything changes. You don't just try harder—you think differently. You don't just behave better—you become someone new.

The mind governed by the Spirit chooses surrender over control. The Spirit does not simply advise; He inhabits. He does not merely convict; He empowers. He does not stand beside the path of repentance pointing forward—He lives within you, supplying the strength you need for every step.

Repentance is not sustained by guilt. It's not maintained by religious effort. Radical, lasting repentance is the fruit of a Spirit-transformed mind. It is not forced behavior. It is the natural result of a new mind and a new nature. The old man may resist, but the Spirit keeps drawing us into life.

When God places His Spirit within a person, the transformation is not superficial. It does not depend on fear, or guilt, or spiritual adrenaline. It rests entirely on divine indwelling. The Spirit renews the mind, redirects the will, and produces the kind of repentance that endures—not because we are strong, but because He is present.

Daily Repentance Is Spirit-Fueled Surrender

But the flesh doesn't die quietly. It must be crucified daily. Repentance is a way of life, a daily turning, and daily surrender. The flesh rises every morning with new demands—new justifications, new excuses, new temptations. That's why daily repentance requires more than resolve. It requires the Spirit.

The Holy Spirit doesn't bulldoze His way into your habits. He whispers and nudges. The Spirit convicts—but He does not coerce. He empowers—but He does not override the will. He speaks—but He does not shout. To live a life of repentance, we must choose to listen. We must choose to yield. We must choose to walk away from the patterns of the flesh and into the freedom of the Spirit.

But that kind of surrender is not easy. There are obstacles. There are barriers. There are quiet lies we believe and subtle comforts we cling to that keep us from repenting at all. If repentance is so urgent, so beautiful, and so Spirit-driven, why do so many of us resist it?

Let's talk about what gets in the way.

How Do We Experience Radical Repentance?

Radical repentance doesn't happen by accident. Repentance begins with awareness — an awakened understanding of sin. We cannot repent of what we refuse to see. Repentance acknowledges our wrongdoings, takes responsibility for our actions, and makes amends where possible.

Repentance is not just regret. It is much more than saying we're sorry. It is a deep recognition of the harm we've caused, the holiness we've offended, and the distance we've created between ourselves and God. This kind of repentance does not simply grieve over what we've done. It longs to become someone new. It changes direction, not just intention. Repentance deeply transforms our lives through the power of the Spirit, redirecting our hearts, reshaping our desires, and setting us on a new path toward God.

Repentance requires the acknowledgment that we have disobeyed God. We violated His law, offended His moral purity, and arrogantly disregarded His divine authority. This realization doesn't come from looking at others. It comes when we stop deceiving ourselves.

We often excuse our sin by comparison. We tell ourselves we're not as bad as someone else. We grade our failures on a sliding scale. But God does not rank sin the way we do. He is not swayed by severity or scandal. He is concerned with sin itself.

In the eyes of God, the gossiper is just as culpable as the murderer. The pornographer is equally guilty as the adulterer or anyone who is sexually immoral. The tax fudger is no less a thief than the armed robber. These comparisons are not exaggerations. They are reminders that sin is not measured by how society reacts, but by how God defines holiness.

We fall into the trap of thinking in terms of "big sins." We know what makes headlines—murder, adultery, abuse, addiction. But the sins we commit in secret—outbursts of anger, sarcastic words, bitter thoughts, quiet jealousy—often escape our concern. We excuse them. We call them personality flaws or bad days. We assume God is too busy with the real sinners to be bothered by our smaller transgressions. But in God's eyes, sin is not judged by shock value—it is judged by whether or not it reflects His character. And anything that flows from pride, selfishness, or unbelief—even if unnoticed by others—is a serious matter to a holy God.

We must overcome our deep instinct to rationalize what we know is wrong. We give sin new names. We explain it away. We soothe our conscience while continuing in behavior we know is unrighteous.

But repentance requires more. It demands honesty. It calls us to stop defending our sin and start confessing it for what it is: unrighteous, willful, and offensive to the heart of a holy God. The real challenge lies in recognizing not only the dramatic sins of the past, but the subtle sins of the present—those small, quiet, daily patterns that distance us from the presence of Christ. That is why repentance must become a daily posture. Only the Spirit can help us see what we've learned to overlook—and lead us to surrender what we've quietly accepted for far too long.

The Grief That Leads to Life

Repentance requires more than emotional regret. It requires what Scripture calls godly sorrow. Godly sorrow is a deep, spiritual mourning that awakens when we finally grasp the seriousness of sin. It's not just feeling bad. It's not the panic that rises when we've been caught. It's not the shame that flares when others find out. Godly sorrow is deeper. It is born from the realization that our sin has dishonored the holiness of God and trampled the grace that He so freely offered.

This kind of sorrow does not rise from wounded pride. It rises from reverence. It comes when we begin to understand how deeply God hates sin—not as a matter of preference, but as a matter of His nature.

Godly sorrow deeply regrets actions that dishonor God. This remorse only comes when we understand how God hates sin. God does not hate it as a preference – like some hate Coca-Cola, but love Pepsi. If you're thirsty and Coca-Cola is all you can find, it doesn't matter how loyal you are to Pepsi, you will drink Coca-Cola. God hates sin at His very core. It is not negotiable. He cannot tolerate it.

He cannot overlook it. Sin is fundamentally opposed to His nature. He must judge it, punish it, purge it!

If the cross tells us anything—and it surely does—it tells us how fiercely God hates sin. The death of Christ was not a symbolic gesture or a moral example. It was a blood-soaked judgment on everything unholy. Christ did not die to tidy up minor flaws or polish our image. He died to absorb the full weight of divine wrath against cosmic treason — our willful rejection of the One who made us.

And when we realize how deeply God despises sin—how completely it violates His nature—and how carelessly we have indulged in it, we are forced to confront the uncomfortable truth that our hearts are far more unlike Christ than we dared to believe. That realization is not meant to crush us; it is meant to awaken us. It drives us to our knees—not just in sorrow, but in surrender. When we take the cross seriously, we cannot take sin lightly. That awareness humbles us. It silences our excuses. It exposes the gap between the holiness we admire and the compromise we tolerate.

We mourn because we see how easily we cast aside the price God paid in Christ on our behalf for a momentary indulgence. And yet — even in His anger — God's love still abounds. His Son, Jesus Christ, bore the weight of our sin, not because we were righteous, but precisely because we were not.

Repentance requires a heartfelt appeal to the mercy of God. True repentance always turns upward—away from self-reliance and toward divine grace. We cry out not just for pardon, but for cleansing. In fervent prayer, we ask God to wash our conscience clean. We ask Him to remove the guilt that clings to us and the shame that weighs down our souls. We ask for strength—not just to feel different, but to live differently.

Repentance asks for the power to overcome repetitive sin. Now, let's understand something. Praying for God to help us resist repetitive sins doesn't mean we can just relax. If we sin again, is it God's fault because we prayed and He didn't prevent it? No! Prayer is not a license to return to old patterns. If we sin again, it is not because God failed to deliver. It is often because we failed to prepare and resist.

Repentance includes deep, deliberate thought. It is a conscious examination of our habits, our vulnerabilities, and our routines. We must learn to recognize what leads us down the path of temptation before we are already halfway there. What triggers our sin? What environments weaken our resolve? What people, situations, or thoughts pull us away from the Spirit and back into the flesh?

This is the work of repentance. Not just sorrow, but strategy. Not just emotion, but action.

Scripture calls us to *produce fruit in keeping with repentance.* (Matthew 3:8) That is not a passive process. It is the intentional pursuit of holiness, a daily guarding of the heart, a refusal to flirt with what once enslaved us. We do not return to places we once fell and pretend we are stronger now. We do not stroll into familiar fields of failure and act surprised when we fall again.

Repentance walks with caution, not carelessness. It does not test how close we can come to the edge. It chooses a different path altogether. Not because we are afraid of sin's power, but because we have learned to love the purity of Christ more than the momentary pleasure of compromise.

If repentance is so urgent, so freeing, so essential to the life of faith—why do so many Christians resist it? The truth is, most of us don't deny the need to repent. We simply delay it. We excuse it. We soften its demands until it becomes a suggestion rather than a summons.

What Keeps Christians from Radical Repentance?

One barrier is complacency. We understand that sin is serious. We know that if offends the heart of God and grieves the Spirit. We are also fully aware sin condemns our souls. But we also know God is loving, gracious, and forgiving. We find comfort in knowing we are saved by grace through faith. Or, as Paul so wonderfully explains, *There is no condemnation for those who are in Christ Jesus.* (Romans 8:1)

Over time, that grace becomes something we presume upon. We say things like, "I'll do better," or "God understands." We convince ourselves that since forgiveness is always available, change is always optional. But Scripture never describes grace as permission to stay the same. It is the very power that enables transformation.

Satan loves to twist the truth of grace into a reason to stay stagnant. He whispers that sin is no big deal. That God will forgive you anyway. That your failure is inevitable and your repentance unnecessary. If we believe that lie long enough, we begin to minimize what Christ died to defeat.

Satan wants to convince you that since you are forgiven in Jesus, sin is no big deal. I mean, God is going to forgive you, right? Why should you worry about it? It's just a small mistake. It's not like you are hurting anybody. Satan wants to numb your conscience and normalize disobedience.

And, if we are truthful with ourselves, Satan can be really effective. This thinking was already present before the ink on all the pages of the New Testament was dry. Jude wrote, *They are godless men, who change the grace of our God into a license for immorality.* (Jude 4) Paul asks, *Shall we continue in sin so that grace may abound?* (Romans 6:1) Those statements were not just a warning for the world. They were written for believers in the church. For people who knew the truth, but had grown too comfortable with their sin to confront it.

The struggle is not new, but it remains just as challenging. We haven't become immune to our spiritual sickness. God forgives sin, but sin can't be trivialized. When faced with a difficult temptation, "God will forgive me so I'll go ahead and do it" isn't an appropriate response. The proper response is radical repentance. Cut the cancer of sin from your life!

There is another barrier to radical repentance—one we don't often name out loud. But we need to. Some people are simply too lazy to change. That may sound harsh, but it is true.

Godliness can be hard work. Transformation does not happen by accident. I heard one of my mentors Jonathan Milligan express it this way. "No one can do your pushups for you". There are some things you can't outsource or delegate. Some things you have to do yourself. Becoming like Christ is one of them.

No one can be godly for you. But changing your life is hard. Developing new habits is difficult. Spiritual maturity doesn't come easy, and it doesn't arrive overnight. And some Christians just don't want to put in the work.

Some believers grow so used to their spiritual inertia that they no longer expect real change to happen. So they don't even try. The hard work of godliness feels like too much. So instead, they settle into excuses that sound spiritual but lack surrender. "Well, God knows what I'm like." "God knows I can't resist . . ." "Well, I guess that's just my weakness." Or, even worse, "I guess that's just my cross to bear." As if any kind of sin could be treated as a sacred burden.

But none of these phrases reflect repentance. They reflect resignation. They are not admissions of humility. They are permissions to remain unchanged.

Sometimes, we are just too lazy to be godly. We just don't want to put forth the effort. It is important to remember that God calls us to be transformed and to grow in holiness.

Let's be clear: it is natural to struggle. Every Christian has weaknesses. But Scripture never calls us to accept spiritual stagnation. It calls us to pursue holiness with perseverance, to put off the old self, and to press on toward the upward call of God in Christ Jesus. We are called to actively pursue godliness and make efforts to overcome our weaknesses with the help of the Holy Spirit. God gives us the strength and grace to change and become more like Him, but we must also actively cooperate with His transforming work in our lives. This requires personal responsibility and a willingness to put in the necessary work and effort.

There is no shortcut to godliness. There is no substitute for obedience. And there is no room for laziness in a life shaped by the cross.

There is another barrier to radical repentance—one we're often afraid to admit. Sometimes, we simply enjoy our sin too much to let it go.

That may be difficult to hear. But it's real. Some people won't change because they don't want to. They know what they're doing is wrong. They know it violates God's Word. They know it grieves the Spirit. And still, they choose it—again and again. It's just that simple. The desire for immediate gratification overshadows the desire for radical repentance.

And yet—we must be careful. Not every struggle with repentance is rooted in defiance. People are complex. Behind persistent sin can lie deep wounds: unhealed trauma, addictive patterns, emotional pain, or years of spiritual confusion. Not every refusal to repent is rebellion. Sometimes it's weariness. Sometimes it's fear. Sometimes it's simply a soul that doesn't yet know how to hope for freedom.

So we must speak truth—but we must do it with compassion. We cannot pretend that sin is harmless. But we also cannot assume every sinner is heartless. The goal is not condemnation. The goal is restoration.

Radical repentance does not begin with shame. It begins with surrender. And that surrender becomes possible only when the love of Christ becomes more beautiful to us than the sin we once clung to. Until Jesus is more desirable than our addiction, more satisfying than our indulgence, and more trustworthy than our coping mechanisms, we will keep returning to what destroys us.

That's why repentance is not just about behavior. It is about affection. The call to repent is not just a call to leave sin. It is a call to treasure Christ.

Conclusion: Don't Wait for the Storm to Hit

You don't wait to act when a tornado is coming. You don't sit still, weigh your options, or wonder how close is too close. You move. You run. You get to safety while there's still time. Not because you're scared—but because you're awake.

That's what repentance is. It is the moment the sky shifts and you see the storm for what it is. You realize that sin isn't a small issue. It's not a personality flaw. It's not a minor mess-up. It is the rebellion that nailed Christ to the cross—and the darkness He died to set you free from.

And when you really see it, you stop negotiating. You stop justifying. You stop waiting. You don't delay repentance when you know the truth. You act. You change direction.

You throw yourself into the mercy of God and say, *Create in me a clean heart, O God. Renew a right spirit within me.* (Psalm 51:10)

Radical repentance is not about shame—it's about surrender. It's not fueled by guilt—it's empowered by grace.

It begins with a Spirit-awakened awareness of sin. It deepens with godly sorrow that leads to life. And it endures because the Holy Spirit gives us new desires, a new mind, and a new way to walk.

You may have stumbled. You may have been complacent. You may have let laziness dull your spiritual hunger. You may have loved your sin more than your Savior. But that doesn't have to be the end of your story.

The storm is still coming. But there's still time to move.

Get to the place of safety. Flee to the cross. Let the love of Christ overwhelm the love of sin. Let His Spirit lead you to freedom.

The Road Ahead

Repentance clears the path. Baptism takes the step.

When the heart surrenders, the body must follow. When the mind is renewed, the life must respond. That's why the road doesn't end with conviction—it leads to immersion.

Repentance turns from sin. Baptism unites with Christ.

The early church never separated the two. Those who heard the gospel, believed it, and repented of their sins were baptized—immediately, publicly, unmistakably. Not as a ritual. Not as a symbol. As a burial. As a birth. As a bold union with the crucified and risen Lord.

In the next chapter, we'll enter those waters. We'll see why baptism is not an add-on to salvation. It's a turning point. A spiritual death and resurrection. A moment where grace and faith collide in sacred surrender.

You've turned toward God. Now it's time to be buried with Christ—and rise to walk a brand-new road.

Baptism

A Simple Act, A Sacred Reality

More Than a Splash

B aptism appears to be such a simple act. A person immersed in water and raised up. It doesn't look unique, or special, or exciting, or mystical, or spiritual. It reminds me of a trip we took to a waterpark as a family. DiAnne, Houston, and Ry like waterparks. Me, not so much. I don't swim very well. I can't float or tread water, and I don't like to be underwater. The thought of careening at blazing speed through an enclosed tube and being unceremoniously dumped into a pool of water terrifies me. I'm afraid I would become disoriented, swallow a mouthful of water, and drown in the kiddie pool. So, on that particular afternoon, I stood at the end of the water slide watching people plummet into a pool of water. On one hand, I was watching for members of my family, and on the other hand, I was secretly watching to see if anyone was as terrified as I would have been. Then, my evangelistic preacher training kicked in. What if I stood at the pool of water and said, "In the name of the Father, Son, and Holy Spirit, I baptize you in the name of Jesus for the forgiveness of your sin."? I could probably baptize a couple of hundred people in an afternoon! I would be a world-renowned evangelist.

That plan has a major flaw, doesn't it? The people casually dumped into that pool of water would not have any idea they were making a commitment to Jesus. And, if they were not consciously making a commitment to Jesus, there would be no conversion. They would just be getting wet.

What makes baptism special? Why isn't it just like the end of the waterslide, jumping off a diving board, falling out of a kayak, or any other activity where one is intentionally or unintentionally immersed in water? Is there "special" water at church? No. It's regular water. Is it location? No. You can be baptized anywhere. You aren't required to be baptized in a church building. Is it the baptismal clothes people wear? No. You can be baptized in ordinary, every-day clothes. Is it the preacher? No. Anyone can baptize you. So what makes baptism special? What makes baptism sacred?

God does. Your faith in Jesus makes it extraordinary. The gift of the Holy Spirit makes it phenomenal. Although it seems ordinary from a physical viewpoint, baptism is re-markable from a spiritual viewpoint. Baptism signifies our commitment to Jesus. Baptism supernaturally connects a believer to the death, burial, and resurrection of Jesus. It is wonderful, mysterious, and exciting.

Baptism is Jesus' plan for those who believe in Him. Bap-tism is not merely a tradition passed down through gen-erations—it is a command given by Jesus Himself. After His resurrection, He spoke directly to His disciples and charged them with a mission that would carry His message to the ends of the earth. *Go and make disciples of all nations, baptizing them in the name of the Father and of the Son and of the Holy Spirit, teaching them to obey everything I have commanded you.* (Matthew 28:19-20). This was not a suggestion or an optional ritual. It was part of the divine blueprint for those who would believe in Him.

The Baptism of Jesus

Jesus didn't just command baptism. He lived it. Before Jesus ever commanded His followers to be baptized, He first submitted to baptism Himself. Before Jesus ever preached a sermon or healed a sick body, He walked into the Jordan River. Jesus instructed John the Baptist to baptize Him as an example for those who would believe in Him.

Then Jesus came from Galilee to the Jordan to John, to be baptized by him. John would have prevented him, saying, "I need to be baptized by you, and do you come to me?" But Jesus answered him, "Let it be so now, for thus it is fitting for us to fulfill all righteousness." Then he consented. (Matt. 3:13–15)

John the Baptist recognized the strangeness of this request. He knew Jesus was sinless. He knew that if anyone should be performing a baptism that day, Jesus should be baptizing him. But Jesus insisted. Not for show. Not for spectacle. But for righteousness.

Jesus did not step into the Jordan because He needed cleansing. He was not baptized to repent or to be forgiven. He had no sin of His own to confess or lay down. From His birth to His death, Jesus lived in perfect obedience to the Father. Every thought, every motive, every action was holy.

The book of Hebrews affirms this with unwavering clarity: *He was tempted in every way, just as we are—yet He did not sin.* (Hebrews 4:15).

So why did Jesus insist on being baptized?

He was baptized to fulfill God's plan. He was baptized to identify with us in our need, even though He Himself had no need. He was baptized to inaugurate the ministry that would ultimately take Him to the cross. In that moment, He stood in the water where sinners stood, not as one who needed redemption, but as the one who would provide it.

Though Jesus had no sin of His own, He came to carry the weight of ours. As Paul later explained, *God made Him who had no sin to be sin for us, so that in Him we might become the righteousness of God.* (2 Corinthians 5:21). That does not mean Jesus became sinful, nor does it suggest that He ever disobeyed the Father. It means that He willingly bore the burden of human sin. He was treated as if He were guilty so that we could be treated as if we were righteous. He took our place so we could be given His.

The baptism of Jesus was not a private event. It was a divine announcement. When Jesus came up from the water, the heavens opened. The Holy Spirit descended like a dove and landed on Him. A voice from heaven announced, *This is my beloved Son, in whom I am well pleased.* (Matthew 3:17). This was the public affirmation of Jesus as the Messiah, the Son of God, and the Savior of the world. It marked the beginning of His ministry and foreshadowed the mission He would complete through His death, burial, and resurrection.

The Beginning of New Life

But that moment pointed forward as well. It foreshadowed the outpouring of the Spirit that would later be offered to every believer. When Peter preached to the crowd at Pentecost, he echoed this very reality: *Repent and be baptized, every one of you, in the name of Jesus Christ for the forgiveness of your sins, and you will receive the gift of the Holy Spirit.* (Acts 2:38). Just as the Spirit came upon Jesus at His baptism, so the Spirit comes to dwell within every believer who responds in faith.

Baptism publicly proclaims our faith in Jesus and marks the beginning of our new life in Him. It is not merely a symbolic act or religious gesture. Baptism transcends being just a sign. It is a moment of spiritual formation—a holy threshold through which we pass from death into life. It is the beginning of a transformation, the crossing over into a new realm of existence. Through baptism, we leave behind the old world of sin and death and enter the new world of righteousness and life in Christ.

This new life is not generated by personal resolve or moral improvement. It originates from Christ alone. His death on the cross, offered as a sacrifice for our sin, provides the righteousness we could never earn. His burial signified the end of fleshly temptation and the silencing of sin's accusations. His resurrection defeated death itself and removed the penalty our sin deserved. In baptism, God unites us with those life-altering events. We are joined with Christ, not in metaphor only, but in divine reality. Baptism does not derive its significance from what we do in that moment—it is significant because of what God does. It is not a work we perform. It is a sacred act of grace, where faith receives what God has promised.

Buried and Raised with Christ

What shall we say, then? Shall we continue to sin so that grace may increase? By no means! We died to sin; how can we live in it any longer? Or don't you know that all of us who were baptized into Christ Jesus were baptized into his death? We were therefore buried with him through baptism into death in order that, just as Christ was raised from the dead through the glory of the Father, we too may live a new life. If we have been united with him like this in his death, we will certainly also be united with him in his resurrection. For we know that our old self was crucified with him so that the body of sin might be done away with, that we should no longer be slaves to sin— because anyone who has died has been freed from sin. Now if we died with Christ, we believe that we will also live with him. For we know that since Christ was raised from the dead, he cannot die again; death no longer has mastery over him. The death he died, he died to sin once for all; but the life he lives, he lives to God. In the same way, count yourselves dead to sin but alive to God in Christ Jesus. Therefore do not let sin reign in your mortal body so that you obey its evil desires. Do not offer the parts of your body to sin, as instruments of wickedness, but rather offer yourselves to God, as those who have been brought from death to life; and offer the parts of your body to him as instruments of righteousness. For sin shall not be your master, because you are not under law, but under grace. (Romans 6:1–14)

Paul begins Romans 6 with a piercing question that every believer must wrestle with: *What shall we say then? Shall we continue in sin that grace may abound?* (Romans 6:1). If salvation is by grace, and grace increases where sin is present, then should we keep on sinning to make more room for grace?

Paul does not entertain that logic for a moment. Paul's response is immediate and emphatic. *By no means!* The idea is unthinkable. If we have truly died to sin, how can we continue living in it? Grace does not give us permission to stay the same. It gives us the power to become new.

Paul then turns to baptism as the foundational proof of this transformation. *Do you not know that all of us who have been baptized into Christ Jesus were baptized into his death?* Baptism is not a ceremonial act. It is a death sentence for the old self. When we are baptized, we are not simply making a decision to follow Jesus. We are being united with Him in His death, burial, and resurrection.

The word Paul uses is deliberate: *into*. Not beside Christ. Not near Christ. We are baptized *into* Christ. Baptism places us *in* Him. That union changes everything. In baptism, I am no longer defined by who I was. I am now identified with the One who died and rose again. Whatever happened to Christ—His death, His burial, His resurrection—has, in a spiritual sense, happened to me. Baptism is not merely symbolic. It reflects a supernatural transformation where the believer is joined to the Savior. In that moment, the old life ends. A new life begins. And everything about who I am is now rooted in Him.

Set Free From the Old Self

We are baptized into Christ's death. That is not just a well-tuned phrase. It is a spiritual reality. When Jesus died on the cross, something more than physical suffering took place. That death was the final break between the sinless Son and the world of temptation. Christ had lived among us, clothed in human flesh, exposed to every temptation that we face. Though He never sinned, He was constantly pursued by sin's voice. It whispered in the wilderness. It hissed through the crowds. It prowled in the shadows of every choice. But He resisted it perfectly. Not once did He surrender to its power.

Yet even for the sinless Son, temptation remained present. It pressed on Him. It surrounded Him. But when He died, all of that came to an end. Sin's voice fell silent. The enemy lost all access. The body that had once been a target for attack was laid down in death. And with that death, the last foothold of temptation was severed. Sin no longer had any claim. Its reach ended where the grave began.

That is the death we are baptized into.

In Christ, we do not simply escape sin's penalty. We are delivered from its power. We share in a death that broke temptation's grip. When we are united with Christ in baptism, we are joined to that decisive moment—the moment when sin's pursuit was cut off and its authority was undone.

That is why Paul can say with such boldness *We know that our old self was crucified with Him so that the body of sin might be brought to nothing, so that we would no longer be enslaved to sin.* (Romans 6:6). The cross was not just the place where sin was punished. It was the place where sin's voice was silenced.

And just as death broke the power of temptation over Christ, so our burial with Him in baptism marks the final seal on that separation.

We are not only baptized into Christ—we are buried with Him. Paul writes, *We were therefore buried with him by baptism into death, in order that, just as Christ was raised from the dead through the glory of the Father, we too might walk in newness of life.* (Romans 6:4). The imagery is unmistakable. Baptism is not a light sprinkling of change. It is a complete immersion into death. The old self does not gradually fade. It is laid to rest.

There is a reason baptism is not described as a drizzle or symbolic washing. It is called a burial. It mirrors the grave. When you go down into the water, you are identifying with Jesus in the most profound way. Just as Christ's body was lowered into the tomb, your former life is lowered into that watery grave. This is not a casual gesture—it is a deliberate, decisive act of surrender. The old habits, the old loyalties, the old patterns of thought—everything that once defined you apart from Christ—is buried and left behind. Past regrets, failures, and mistakes are buried. The water closes over you like the tomb sealed Christ away. It's a powerful picture of complete surrender.

We do not partially bury the past. We do not halfway surrender to Jesus. You don't half-bury someone. You don't halfway die. Baptism is total. It marks the end of one existence and the beginning of another. In that moment, Christ's death becomes your death. The old self is crucified. The record of your sins is nailed to the cross. And the life that once lived in slavery to sin is sealed away in the grave.

But the story does not end in the grave.

Jesus did not remain in the tomb. On the third day, He rose—body intact, breath restored, glory revealed. Death could not hold Him, and the grave had no power to keep Him. His resurrection was not just a return to life. It was the beginning of a new creation. He was raised by the glory of the Father, and in that moment, all things began to be made new.

In baptism, we are joined to that same resurrection. We do not rise from the water unchanged. We rise with Christ. We rise into a new way of living. Just as we were united with Him in death, we are now united with Him in life. The old self was crucified. The new self is raised—not simply improved, but reborn.

Paul says it plainly: *If we have been united with Him in a death like His, we shall certainly be united with Him in a resurrection like His*. (Romans 6:5). The resurrection of Jesus becomes the resurrection of the believer. Not just in some future sense, but in the here and now. We rise from the water with a new identity. We walk in newness of life—not as people who try harder, but as people who have been made new.

That is what it means to be alive in Christ. The grave has no hold. The past has no claim. Sin still tempts, but it no longer rules. The resurrection power that raised Jesus from the dead now lives in us. And from that moment on, we do not walk alone. We walk in step with the Spirit, guided by grace, anchored in victory.

This resurrection life is not theoretical. It has real consequences for how we live right now. If we have died with Christ and been raised with Christ, then everything changes. What does that mean for you?

It means your old self—the person you used to be—is no longer in charge.

Paul writes, *We know that our old self was crucified with Him so that the body of sin might be brought to nothing, so that we would no longer be enslaved to sin. For one who has died has been set free from sin.* (Romans 6:6–7). This is not wishful thinking. This is the certainty of the gospel. The old self is not in rehabilitation. It is not under construction. It is crucified. The death of Jesus did not just deal with sin's penalty—it dismantled sin's power.

To be crucified with Christ means that your former identity—the part of you that lived apart from God, that answered to the flesh, that chased desires without restraint—is nailed to the cross. It is not in control anymore. It has no legal standing. It has no authority. Its voice may still echo, but it no longer commands obedience.

Sin still speaks, but it no longer reigns.

The person who has died is free. Just as a deceased person no longer answers to earthly laws, the believer who has died with Christ is no longer under the rule of sin. That body of sin—the flesh that once dictated your every move—is rendered powerless. It may protest. It may scream. But it cannot rule unless you invite it back to the throne.

In baptism, God does more than forgive your sins. He breaks your chains. You are not just pardoned. You are liberated.

This is more than a personal experience. It is a shift in status. Sin no longer defines you. The law no longer condemns you. You have been moved from death to life, from bondage to freedom, from an old self to a new creation. The outcome is already decided. You are alive in Christ.

A Positional Change

In Romans 7:1-6, Paul introduces a legal illustration to describe our new status when we are united with Christ. He begins with a simple truth. The law has authority over a person only as long as that person is alive. That is the way every legal system works. A contract, a debt, an obligation—all of these remain in force while someone is living, but none of them apply once death occurs. Death cancels every claim.

To drive the point home, Paul uses the example of marriage. A woman is legally bound to her husband as long as he lives. But if he dies, she is released. The covenant is no longer in force. The legal bond dissolves. She is free from that relationship because the one holding the claim is no longer alive.

Paul then applies that same truth to our relationship with the law. We were once bound to it. The law ruled over us. It measured us. It exposed our failures. It condemned us. But when we died with Christ, everything changed. That old relationship ended. The law no longer defines who we are or determines where we stand. Through Christ, we entered into a new covenant—not governed by rule-keeping, but shaped by grace. We belong to someone else now.

Paul writes, *So, my brothers, you also died to the law through the body of Christ, that you might belong to another—to Him who was raised from the dead—in order that we might bear fruit to God.* (Romans 7:4). Death freed us, not to live lawlessly, but to live fruitfully. We were not released to run wild. We were released so that we could be joined to Christ and live the kind of life that reflects Him.

The old way was marked by striving and failing, by bearing the weight of rules that could never redeem. That way died when we died with Jesus. The new way began with the resurrection. Now we live by the Spirit. Now we walk in freedom. We no longer measure righteousness by the law. We bear the fruit of righteousness through our union with Christ.

The law was never the problem. Sin was. The law exposed our brokenness, but it could not heal it. It could name the disease, but it could not provide the cure. Christ did what the law never could. He broke sin's hold. He made us new. He didn't just cancel the record against us. He changed our identity. We no longer live under the pressure of rules we can't keep. We live in the power of grace. We are no longer bound to the law. We are bound to Christ.

Forgiven and Clean

On the day of Pentecost when Peter stood before a crowd who had just heard the unthinkable, he didn't sugarcoat the truth. The man they crucified—Jesus of Nazareth—was not a blasphemer or a fraud. He was the Son of God, the Lord and Messiah, now risen from the dead and exalted to the right hand of God. The people were cut to the heart. Their question was urgent, desperate, and sincere: *Brothers, what shall we do?* (Acts 2:37).

Peter didn't hesitate. He didn't invite them to wait or reflect or search their feelings. He gave them a command backed by promise: *Repent and be baptized, every one of you, in the name of Jesus Christ for the forgiveness of your sins. And you will receive the gift of the Holy Spirit.* (Acts 2:38).

In that one sentence, the gospel call is made clear. Two gifts are offered— forgiveness of sins and the Holy Spirit. Two responses are required — repentance and baptism. This is not a private moment of reflection. This is public surrender.

God promises to forgive completely, not symbolically or temporarily. Every sin, every failure, every regret is erased. It isn't covered up. It isn't postponed. It isn't rolled forward to a later time. Every sin is removed. Forgiveness isn't just about clearing a record. It's a full release. The debt is gone. The weight of failure and guilt is lifted. Baptism isn't just a moment; it's the dividing line between who you were and who you can be in Christ.

God gives you a clean slate. David captured it in an image. *For as high as the heavens are above the earth, so great is his love for those who fear him; as far as the east is from the west, so far has he removed our transgressions from us.* (Psalm 103:11-12) Jeremiah prophesied a new covenant. *For I will forgive their wickedness and will remember their sins no more.* (Jeremiah 31:34)

Every year, we pack up our kayaks and head out for a weekend on the water with a close-knit group of friends. We paddle, we laugh, we eat too much, and when it's all over, we settle the costs. Nothing complicated. We divvy up the expenses, pass around the receipts, and write the checks.

One year, DiAnne wrote a check to cover our share. The friend who received it put it on the dash of the truck and didn't think much of it. Two weeks later, she finally got around to making the deposit. But when she pulled out the check, it was blank. No name. No signature. No amount. Just a smooth piece of paper where ink used to be.

She called us, confused and a little amused. "Why did you give me a blank check?"

Turns out, DiAnne had used my Pilot Frixion pen. If you've never used one, here's the catch: the ink disappears when it's exposed to heat. The check had been sitting in a hot truck for days, and the heat had erased every word and number.

That's what happens when God forgives your sin. Picture a massive book filled with everything you've ever done wrong—every sharp word, every lie, every selfish act, every regret. Page after page, it holds the weight of your past. A catalog of failure.

Then, in an instant, it's wiped clean. Not scribbled out. Not hidden under correction tape. Gone.

God doesn't see it. God doesn't hold it against you. Through the blood of Jesus, your sin disappears like Frixion ink under heat. What once was real and condemning is now erased by the grace of God.

That's what baptism marks. The moment when everything that once defined you is wiped away—not delayed, not reduced, not reassigned—but removed.

Filled with the Spirit

God doesn't just take something away—He gives something in return. The same God who removes your sin also fills you with His Spirit. Salvation isn't just subtraction. It's addition. It's not just about what God cancels. It's about what God creates.

When you are baptized into Christ, you don't just walk out washed—you walk out filled. Peter made that clear: *Repent and be baptized . . . for the forgiveness of your sins. And you will receive the gift of the Holy Spirit.* (Acts 2:38). Forgiveness clears the space. The Spirit fills it.

The Holy Spirit provides the fuel for your spiritual journey. He is not a bonus gift for advanced believers. He is the presence of God in you from the moment you rise out of the water. You will learn more about His power and presence in the second book of this series—but make no mistake, He begins His work the moment your new life begins.

God chooses to live in you. The Holy Spirit changes you, empowers you, guides you. The Holy Spirit changes your heart and your desire.

Baptism is not just the start of something new. It is the moment when the curtain is torn, the temple is opened, and the God who once dwelled in holy places chooses to dwell in you, making you His living sanctuary and shaping you into a new creation through His Spirit.

There is no longer distance between you and God. God doesn't choose to live in a church building or a sanctuary. The God who once dwelt in holy places chooses to dwell in you. You are God's temple. You are the holy place. You are the living sanctuary.

The Spirit is not just a presence you feel in worship or a power you sense in prayer. He is the One who shapes your desires, softens your heart, and gives you the strength to live what you believe. He leads, He convicts, He comforts, and He teaches. He changes not just how you act, but who you are.

With the Spirit in you, you don't simply have a new beginning. You become a new creation. The old has gone. The new has come. And that newness is not something you carry alone. It is carried by the God who lives in you.

Clothed in Christ

Have you ever gotten your clothes really dirty? I mean, really dirty. So dirty, the only option was to throw them away. Maybe it was a favorite shirt stained with grease. Maybe it was a pair of pants splattered with paint that wouldn't come out no matter how many times you washed them. Eventually, you realize the truth: you shouldn't try to save what you can't restore. You don't fold it up and put it back in the drawer. You throw it out. It's ruined. It's no longer fit to wear. That was you. Stained beyond usability. And nothing you could do would remove the stain. The stain of sin ruined you. You were dirty beyond redemption.

Sin did not simply leave behind a mark that time or effort could erase. It penetrated to the heart of who you were. It sank deep into your heart and stained your soul. No earthly remedy could help. You could not scrub it off through good behavior or wash it away with sincere intentions. No spiritual detergent could lift it. No effort to patch or disguise it could make it acceptable. The damage was not surface-level. It was complete. You weren't just dirty; you were defiled. You were unfit to stand before a holy God. The guilt and shame pressed down on you, and no human hands could fix it.

Now, imagine putting on a crisp, new shirt and fresh pants. The old, stained clothes are tossed aside. A clean, new set that shines with confidence replaces them. Most people love wearing new clothes. They feel great and confident in their fresh outfits. It's as if they've been reborn, leaving their old selves behind. The excitement is overwhelming, like unwrapping a long-awaited gift on a special occasion.

Paul used this very imagery when he described what happens in baptism. *For all of you who were baptized into Christ have clothed yourselves with Christ.* (Galatians 3:27). This is a declaration of identity. In baptism, you are not only cleansed—you are clothed. You do not step out of the water as someone partially restored. You rise wrapped in the righteousness of Jesus.

The old garments—stained by sin and heavy with shame—are laid aside. They are not stored in the closet. They are thrown out. They no longer define you. And in their place, Christ becomes your covering. His righteousness surrounds you. His honor is now your name. His purity becomes your presentation. You are not dressed in self-improvement. You are clothed in salvation.

The imagery is incredible. You took off your old clothes of sin and shame and put on Christ, your new clothes of righteousness and honor. You are ready for the party!

Something else happens in baptism—something deeper than the outward act and more profound than what the eyes can see. Peter speaks to this mystery in his first letter: *Corresponding to that, baptism now saves you—not the removal of dirt from the flesh, but an appeal to God for a good conscience—through the resurrection of Jesus Christ.* (1 Peter 3:21). The phrase *corresponding to that* refers to Noah's flood. During that time, water was both a tool for judgment and a means of deliverance. For those who rejected God, the flood brought destruction. Noah and his family obeyed God and entered the ark. The water then brought them salvation. It lifted them above judgment and safely guided them to a new start.

Peter makes it clear that baptism is not about washing the body or cleansing the skin. Baptism isn't a bath. It isn't the removal of physical dirt which saves you. It removes the spiritual dirt. Baptism provides a spiritual reality with a physical act.

So Which is It? Both!

Peter's statement in 1 Peter 3:21 centers on a key phrase: *an appeal to God for a good conscience.* This phrase has been translated in different ways. Some versions render it as *appeal,* while others use the word *pledge.* Both translations capture important truths, and both deserve thoughtful attention.

What does it mean to appeal to God for a good conscience in baptism? And what does it mean to pledge a good conscience toward Him? It's the same verse viewed through two lenses. So which is it? Is baptism our appeal to God for a clear conscience? Or is baptism our pledge (promise) to God to have a good conscience?

Let's slow down and read this passage both ways.

Let's begin with the first way to read Peter's phrase: *Baptism is an appeal to God for a good conscience.* This translation frames baptism as a cry for help. It is a desperate plea asking God to cleanse, to forgive, to make things right inside. It's humble, dependent, and God-centered. This reading shifts the weight off human effort and places it fully on God's initiative. It is not our vow to live godly, but our recognition that we can't live at all without Him.

We have nothing to offer. We certainly cannot offer a clean conscience. Remember our core verse? *We are saved by grace though faith - and this is not from yourselves, it is the gift of God – not by works, so that no one can boast.* A changed life does not begin with our promise to do better. It begins with God's promise to make us new.

That's why many translations favor this interpretation. It is the objective reading that emphasizes what God does rather than what a person does. It focuses on divine action, not human resolve. In this view, baptism becomes the prayer of the broken: "God, make me new." It reflects a desperate, deep, and honest cry to God for help with the unshakable trust that God alone has the power to answer it.

Let's explore the second way to read Peter's phrase: *Baptism is the pledge of a good conscience before God*. This translation frames baptism as a promise. It emphasizes what the baptized person is declaring. Baptism is a moment of holy resolve. The person being baptized says, "Because You saved me, I now live for You."

It does not suggest that we earn salvation by making a promise. It simply recognizes that those who are transformed by mercy will respond to mercy with commitment. Many translations lean toward this subjective reading because it captures the relational nature of faith: God saves, and the believer responds with loyalty, integrity, and obedience. Baptism isn't just immersion in water. Baptism is a moment of surrender and resolve.

It is a vow we make from a renewed heart. It's about our response to grace. We make a vow to walk in the light. The emphasis is on what the person being baptized is declaring or doing rather than what God is doing in the moment. We make a deliberate, public decision to serve God with a clean heart.

The believer commits to live obediently to the salvation they have received. It is relational. God saves, and the believer responds with loyalty and integrity. It is similar to a wedding vow. "With this ring, I thee wed, and promise to love and cherish you until death parts us." The ring doesn't create the love or the vow. It is a symbol of the love and the vow. But the speaker makes a pledge, a vow, a commitment. And the vow spoken in that moment becomes the pledge that shapes every day that follows.

So, baptism symbolizes cleansing and commitment. The believer says, "Because you saved me, I now live for You. I will keep my clean conscience clean before you." This interpretation does not deny the grace of God. It affirms it. It simply highlights the natural response of a heart that has been touched by that grace. Baptism, in this view, is not only about cleansing. It is about commitment.

What does Peter mean by *clean conscience*? Does that mean we will never experience guilt or struggle with regret? Of course not. A clean conscience does not mean a sinless life. It does not mean we will never fail, never grieve, or never wrestle with weakness. It means something deeper and more enduring.

A *clean conscience* is the result of Christ's cleansing work and our continued walk in truth. It begins with what He has done—washing us clean through His blood—and continues as we choose to walk in honesty, humility, and obedience before Him. It is not about pretending to be righteous. It is about living openly, without hidden shame, because Christ has carried the full weight of our sin.

Your heart is fully exposed before God. And God, who fully knows your heart, fully accepts you by the cleansing nature of faith in Christ. Because of forgiveness found in Christ, your heart no longer condemns you. Paul says it best, *There is no condemnation for those who are in Christ Jesus.* (Romans 8:1) That is the foundation of a good conscience—not that we are flawless, but that we are forgiven. Not that we are sinless, but that we are covered. Baptism marks that reality. It is the outward sign of an inward surrender. It is the place where we stop clinging to sin, stop performing for approval, and start living honestly with God and ourselves.

Not Just Water

The water doesn't save by magic. It's not just a traditional ritual. It's not about external cleansing. First, it's our inner plea and cry, "God, make me clean." Second, it's our firm vow, "I will live to honor You."

Both interpretations carry truth. Baptism is a cry for mercy and a commitment to walk in that mercy. It is both God's gift and our response. It begins with what God does for us and continues with what we offer back to Him. We do not choose between appeal and pledge. We embrace both, because salvation is not a transaction—it is a relationship. In baptism, the believer enters into that relationship fully—washed by grace, clothed in Christ, filled with the Spirit, and resolved to walk with a conscience made clean by the blood of Jesus.

Let's rewind to the beginning of this chapter—back to that moment at the end of the waterslide. Baptism isn't just about getting dunked. It's not magical water. It's not meaningful without God's grace and your faith meeting in that sacred moment. You can't treat baptism like a spiritual shortcut or loophole to bypass obedience. It's not a bargaining chip, and it certainly doesn't put God in your debt. You don't step out of the water and say, "Okay God, I did my part—now You owe me." That's not how salvation works. Baptism isn't a fast-pass to heaven or a get-out-of-judgment-free card. Without faith, it's just a splash. Without surrender, it's just water.

That's why it's not enough to point to a moment in the past and say, "Well, he was baptized." Maybe he was. But if that baptism wasn't joined to a surrendered heart and an obedient life, it does not carry the spiritual weight we often want it to. Baptism is not just a date on a calendar. It is the beginning of a new creation. It is the line between the old and the new. It is a moment of death, burial, and resurrection.

Summary

Baptism is a matter of obedience. It is about honoring what God has commanded, even when we don't fully understand all the mystery wrapped inside it. Years ago, I had a friend who spent years wrestling with this very thing. We talked. We prayed. We circled around questions that came slowly, sometimes weeks apart. Then one day, while we were fishing, he said, "I got it figured out." I said, "You got what figured out?" He said, "Baptism. I know why it matters." I asked, "What did you decide?" And he answered, "Because God said to do it. That's the answer. We are baptized because God said to."

That may sound simple—but it isn't shallow. It's faith in action. Obedience rooted in trust. Baptism is not just about what we feel. It's about what God has revealed.

Though it may seem simple, baptism encompasses a wealth of spiritual significance. Baptism marks a believer's profound transformation and union with Christ. Through baptism, God's grace purifies inwardly, making baptism a cherished cornerstone of faith. As God's grace purifies, the believer makes a commitment to honor God with his life. Baptism incorporates both spiritual reality and physical symbol. Water is not the cause of salvation, but a picture. It is a public acknowledgment, a public confession, and an aqueduct to connect God's grace and the believer's commitment.

It is not a formality. It is a holy moment. It is not about religious performance. It is about being born again.

When we are baptized, we do not simply get wet. We are buried with Christ, raised to walk in newness of life, and clothed with His righteousness. And we do it for one reason: because God said to.

Baptism marks the beginning—but not the end. It is the starting line of a new life, not the finish. Rising from the water, we are not only forgiven and filled—we are called to live differently. What follows baptism is not spiritual autopilot, but a daily journey of devotion. The next stretch of the road is shaped by piety—not a show of religion, but a sincere walk of faith, fueled by grace, and formed by the Spirit who now lives within us.

The Road Ahead

Baptism is not the finish line. It's the first step out of the grave.

You rise from the water washed, filled, and free—but not finished. Forgiveness is the foundation, not the whole structure. Being clothed in Christ is the beginning of becoming like Him. You've stepped into a new life. Now it's time to walk it.

And that walk has a name: piety.

Not the plastic or polished kind that poses for approval. Not the stiff, hollow routines of religion. Piety is real. Piety is lived. It is the visible evidence of the invisible grace now pulsing through your soul. It is what happens when belief becomes behavior, when reverence becomes routine, when holiness invades the ordinary.

You've been saved by grace. You've been buried with Christ. Now the question is: Will you live for Him?

The next chapter is not about checking boxes or measuring moral output. It's about a life reoriented around the presence of God. It's about habits formed by the Spirit. It's about worship in the quiet places, obedience in the small choices, and the kind of faithfulness that doesn't need an audience.

Baptism began the journey. Piety is how you stay on the road.

Piety

Driving Like You Belong

When I was a sophomore in college in the fall of 1982, I bought a 1967 Ford Mustang. It was lime-gold metallic, 200 inline six engine, 3-speed manual transmission, no air-conditioning, no power brakes and no power steering. It had a deluxe interior with a polished aluminum dash, floor console, and map console. I still have it. During those years, it sat in carports and barns. There were years it wasn't roadworthy and couldn't be driven. It just sat. DiAnne and I have had nicer cars, faster cars, bigger cars. But that old Mustang has a special place in my heart.

Several years ago, I decided to rebuild it. Honestly, I probably should have hauled it to the junkyard. But my heart wouldn't let me. I can't do body work, so Bobby Hunter and his crew of restorers fixed the body and painted it. Bobby rebuilt the engine and the transmission. Then it came back to me. No fenders. No doors. No interior. No windows. No suspension. No wiring. It was nothing more than the frame of a car, stripped bare and suspended on four jack stands in the quiet of the garage.

Now, it's a different color. It has road-racing suspension. It has air conditioning, leather seats, and power brakes. It is wired for electric-assist steering. It has been completely restored. It took about three years for me to transform it from a shell to a completed car. A professional could have done it faster — and better. But, I wanted to do it myself.

I did one small thing every day. Some days I worked longer. But most of the time, I just did one thing every evening after work. Just one small thing. Nobody had to make me do it. I wanted to do it. Nobody had to get me excited for the next thing. I stayed excited. I WANTED to do it. I was passionate about doing it.

What is Piety, Really?

Piety isn't a word often used. Piety is a strong belief in a religion that is shown in the way someone lives. Our belief is that Jesus is the Son of God. In other words, our lifestyle reflects our belief in Jesus. Piety is all the good things our faith in Jesus compels us to do. We might also use words like devoutness or godliness to describe piety. Doing the right thing based on our faith in Jesus is the simplest way to define piety. Piety results from passion.

I poured myself into that Mustang because I loved it. I studied every curve, chased every detail, and gave my time without being asked. I live for Jesus, but not out of guilt, not out of fear, not to earn what I've already been given. I live for Him because He captured my heart. He rescued what was rusted and ruined and made it new. Piety originates from devotion, not duty. It is passion.

So far, we have covered the road to salvation. We believe in Jesus. And that belief manifests itself in several ways.

We confess Jesus is the Son of God by our words and our lifestyle. Confession is more than just saying "I believe Jesus is the Son of God." Confession includes living like Jesus is the Son of God. That is piety. We repent of our sin. Simply put, our faith in Jesus prevents us from doing things of which Jesus doesn't approve or compels us to do things of which He does approve. That is piety. And we are baptized. We are united by baptism to the death, burial, and resurrection of Jesus. We are new creatures. We have a new perspective on life. We have new priorities. That is piety. Piety is the natural expression of our faith. Piety is genuine when it is anchored in commitment and covenant to Christ. It's difficult to consistently do the right thing for the wrong reason.

The War Within

After conversion, we come face-to-face with a significant challenge. We want to quit doing bad things, but temptation overcomes. We want to start doing good things, but we struggle with consistency. If we died to sin, why do we still feel the temptation to sin? You might think "If I died to sin, I shouldn't feel the temptation to sin any longer. What is wrong with me? I don't feel dead to sin."

Nothing is wrong with you. You are completely normal.

We know that the law is spiritual; but I am unspiritual, sold as a slave to sin. I do not understand what I do. For what I want to do I do not do, but what I hate I do. And if I do what I do not want to do, I agree that the law is good. As it is, it is no longer I myself who do it, but it is sin living in me. I know that nothing good lives in me, that is, in my flesh. For I have the desire to do what is good, but I cannot carry it out. For what I do is not the good I want to do; no, the evil I do not want to do—this I keep on doing. Now if I do what I do not want to do, it is no longer I who do it, but it is sin living in me that does it. So I find this law at work: When I want to do good, evil is right there with me. For in my inner being I delight in God's law; but I see another law at work in the members of my body, waging war against the law of my mind and making me a prisoner of the law of sin at work within my members. What a wretched man I am! Who will rescue me from this body of death? Thanks be to God—through Jesus Christ our Lord! So then, I myself in my mind am a slave to God's law, but in the flesh a slave to the law of sin. (Romans 7:14–25)

Before we dive too deep into this subject, read the last couple of verses again. *What a wretched man I am! Who will rescue me from this body of death? Thanks be to God — through Jesus Christ our Lord!* Don't become so discouraged in your struggle that you forget the confidence provided for you in Christ. Jesus came to deliver you from every struggle that troubles you! That is the joy of salvation!

You are no longer a slave to sin. But that doesn't mean sin is eradicated. As long as we are in this body, we will struggle with sin. The new and the old live in constant conflict. Paul revealed with genuine transparency his struggle to meet the radical demands of faith. Paul was drawing from the ache of his own struggle to show this sobering truth: when a believer tries to fight sin without leaning fully on the Spirit of God, defeat isn't just likely—it's inevitable.

Those who live according to the flesh think about the things of the flesh; but those who live in accordance with the Spirit think the things of the Spirit. (Romans 8:5)

So I say, live by the Spirit, and you will not gratify the desires of the flesh. For the flesh desires what is contrary to the Spirit, and the Spirit what is contrary to the flesh. They are in conflict with each other, so that you do not do what you want. (Galatians 5:16-17)

Tune In

The Christian must stay tuned to the correct frequency — the Spirit's frequency. Think of a radio station. Let's assign a random frequency: 104.5. If you have an FM radio and you tune to that frequency, you will hear that station (if you are in range of the signal). For our illustration, the Spirit has no limit on the range of its signal. That station is always broadcasting at 104.5. But if you aren't tuned in, you cannot hear it. The station is still broadcasting, but you are on a different frequency. You will hear another station. Christians must stay tuned in to the Spirit. If not, we will hear another station, another voice. And that voice will be Satan's voice.

But the flesh and the Spirit live in constant conflict. The more we are tuned in to the Spirit; the easier it is to resist sin. As the Spirit's signal loses reception, the more we fall into sin. Piety results from being in tune to the Spirit.

A deep connection exists between Romans 6 (the passage we explored in detail in the previous chapter) and Romans

7. In Romans 6, Paul wrote we are *dead to sin*. Most of the time, I don't feel dead to sin. In Romans 7, Paul wrote *the sin living in me*. That's how I often feel. I feel that sin is very much alive in me. So which is it? Am I dead to sin or does sin live in me? The answer is yes. You are dead to sin. And sin lives in you. You are dead to sin, but the desire to sin isn't dead. That's a head-scratcher, isn't it?

A deep, volatile struggle exists between our flesh and our spirit. Human beings exist in two natures: physical and spiritual; flesh and spirit. If we depend on our flesh, we experience failure. We must rely on the power of the Spirit for victory. Sanctification is a gradual process. It is marked by peaks and valleys. It is like the ebb and flow of the ocean. On top of the wave one second. In the trough of the waves the next. Progress is a series of failures and victories, sinful acts and godly acts. The believer is spiritually aligned to Christ. In principle, the believer is dead to sin. But the believer still encounters and battles sin's presence. Christ provides victory over sin, but the believer still struggles to overcome sin.

Let's take a moment to review our positional change in Jesus. We are dead to sin because we no longer serve sin. Sin is no longer our master, but sin is still our nemesis. Second, we are dead to sin because of the sacrifice of Jesus. *For what the law was powerless to do in that it was weakened by the flesh, God did by sending his own Son in the likeness of flesh to be a sin offering. And so he condemned sin in flesh, in order that the righteous requirements of the law might be fully met in us, who do not live according to the flesh but according to the Spirit.* (Romans 8:3-4) Sin produces death because of the transgression of the law. Every requirement of the law is fulfilled in us because of our relationship to Jesus by faith. Therefore, sin has no power over us.

So, does sin matter? Yes! We cannot live in something to which we died. Forgiveness and grace aren't an excuse to justify sin. Using forgiveness and grace to justify sin is like skating on thin ice. Most likely, tragedy is close. Let me explain.

Don't Skate on Thin Ice

Suppose you are faced with a sin or not-sin decision. You pick the sin. Pick one with which you usually struggle. How about this logic? "I know I shouldn't do this, but I really want to. I know God doesn't want me to. I know it's an ungodly thing. But, I REALLY want to. I'll just go ahead and do it; then, I'll ask God to forgive me. God will forgive me, and I'll try not to do it again. Everything will be fine." That is thin ice. It's thin ice because of the intentionality of sin.

If we are honest with ourselves, there is intentionality to most sin. There are very few sins that are the product of ignorance. For example, we lie. If we didn't know it was a sin to lie, our sin would be unintentional. However, most of the time we have a good grasp on whether an action is a sin or not. We lie, but we know lying is wrong. We just decide to do it anyway. Intentional sin based on future forgiveness grieves God. It grieves God's Spirit.

Piety is our passion to do godly things. Piety is our passion to say "No" to ungodly things. Paul wrote, *For the grace of*

God that bring salvation has appeared to all men. It teaches us to say "No" to ungodliness and worldly passion, and to live self-controlled, upright and godly lives in this present age. (Titus 2:11-12)

Grace doesn't create desire to sin. Grace doesn't provide license to sin. Grace provides passion and motivation to resist sin. Grace creates in us the desire to please God. It produces the passion for a holy life. That is piety.

Piety is faith in action. Piety results from our transformation from old creature to new creature. Faith and grace challenge behavior. That is piety.

While she was listening to Jesus teaching, a woman exclaimed, *Blessed is the womb that gave you birth and the breasts that you nursed.* Jesus gave a simple, direct reply. *Blessed rather are the ones hearing the word of God and keeping it.* (Luke 11:27-28) Jesus was talking about piety, putting our faith into practice.

It isn't enough just to hear God's word. For example, we can open our Bibles and read how we should love others. That is knowledge, and it is good knowledge. But just to know I need to love others isn't adequate. I need to put that knowledge into action. Jesus said, *Love one another. As I have loved you, so you must love one another.* Putting that knowledge into practice creates a challenge. Jesus loved other people even though they didn't love Him back. Jesus loved people who mistreated Him. Jesus loved people who despised Him. Jesus loved people when they only wanted something from Him. Jesus loved people who hated Him. That type of love challenges us. It doesn't come naturally. It is difficult. That is piety: faith in action. Piety is much more comprehensive than just our love for someone. It applies to every area of our life. Jesus said, *Blessed are the ones hearing the Word of God*. But Jesus didn't stop there. He included, *And keeping it.*

Spiritual maturity leads to piety. Spiritual maturity exists when we want what God wants. Our desires must be the same as God's desires. Piety should not be a chore. The closer our relationship with God; the easier piety should be. After we believe in Jesus, we cannot be the same. Do you **have** to serve Jesus or do you **want** to serve Jesus? Do you **want** to honor Jesus or are you **required** to honor Jesus? Our motives and desires change when we become believers in Jesus. It is **want to** vs **have to**.

The Formula

Piety is the result of Desire + Opportunity + Action.

Piety starts with desire. It's a simple question. **What do you want?** Let's make it an open-ended question. Imagine you found a genie bottle, and you get three wishes. You can ask for anything! Maybe you want more money than you think you could ever spend. Maybe you want a house with a pool, a basketball court, a movie theater, 10 bedrooms, and 10 bathrooms. Maybe you want the best-looking man or woman you can imagine. The sky is the limit. What would you ask for? In reality, you have something far more powerful than a genie bottle. You worship a God who created the heavens and the earth with a word. Nothing is impossible for Him. What would you ask for? What is your desire?

Faith in Jesus demands our desire matches exactly what God wants. I can't boil that down to a single ingredient. In fact, it could be and is a thousand different things. It is loving your neighbor as yourself. It is showing compassion and grace. It is fleeing from sin. It is . . . You can fill in the sentence with a plethora of possibilities. But it can be simply defined. As we journey in our spiritual walk, we become more like God. God's desires become our desires.

And we, who with unveiled faces all reflect the Lord's glory, are being transformed into His likeness with ever-increasing glory, which comes from the Lord, who is the Spirit. (2 Corinthians 3:18 NIV)

We reflect God's glory. We are transformed into His likeness. God's heart becomes our desire.

A great biblical example is David. *After removing Saul, he made David their king. He testified concerning him: "I have found David son of Jesse a man after my own heart; he will do everything I want him to do."* (Acts 13:22) What does that mean? David was a man after God's own heart? We might think that David was such a good guy that God really liked him. That God's heart pursued David. That God was thinking, "David is a great guy. I just really like him." What the passage really means is that David wanted to have the heart of God. David pursued God's heart. David wanted to think like God. David wanted to see the world the way God sees the world. David wanted to honor God with every part of his existence. David wanted to have God's heart. That's what we want. Like David, we long to have the heart of God.

Desire creates opportunity.

We start to see opportunity because our observation of the world is altered. When we see the world as God does, something supernatural happens. We want to love. We long to bless. We ache to see others know Jesus. We start noticing things. A weary soul in the back row. A hurting friend who hides behind a smile. A divine interruption in a regular day. An opportunity for a kind word. We recognize those who are enslaved by sin and Satan, and we want to help. It's not that they are worse sinners than we are. They aren't saved sinners. They haven't been redeemed from their empty way of life by the blood of Jesus. We start to see others the way Jesus sees others. Our eyes are opened to the people God puts in our path. God creates holy appointments we would miss if we remain focused on ourselves. Piety isn't just about avoiding sin. Piety is being swept up in the purpose of God. Piety is being available for God. We start observing the ways God can use us in this world.

Desire + opportunity creates action.

Our new observation creates opportunity. We can't just see it. We want to do something about it. That is why piety is a natural expression of faith.

Not only do we recognize God working in the world, we also become more aware of Satan's work in the world. That creates two responses. First, we desire to do the good work of God. We notice the way God works in the world, and we emulate it. Love our neighbor. Show kindness. Help the hurting. Second, we loathe Satan's work in the world. We want to stay far away from sin. God's heart hates sin. So our new heart hates sin. The result? We do good. We despise evil.

Desire + opportunity + action = piety

A dynamic change occurs. We aren't godly because we have to be. We are godly because we want to be. We don't pursue godliness because we're trying to earn something. We pursue godliness because we've already been given everything. Our lives overflow with good works, not out of fear, but out of love.

Let's be clear about something. Piety doesn't save us. It can't and never could. We are saved by God's grace through faith. That has consistently been the theme of this book. But that does not make piety meaningless. It means piety is no longer a desperate attempt to buy God's favor. It becomes a joyful response to the favor we've already received.

It's not a check ledger. Some treat their relationship with God like a spiritual accounting system. Our relationship with God doesn't work like that. It's not if I have one bad behavior, I need two good behaviors. Or, I need to keep a positive balance of good things in relation to bad things. That is flawed logic.

That would lead you to think. "You know, I did 2 really good things this week. I'm entitled to one bad thing this weekend. I think I'll . . ." Or to think, "I did a really bad thing last week, so I need to read my Bible and help my neighbor this week so God still thinks I'm good."

Free to Serve

Good works don't save you, but you can't be saved without them. Good works don't obligate God to save, but good works are a natural expression of faith. The vine produces branches, and the branches bear fruit. Faith without works is not weak. It is dead (James 2:26). And living faith doesn't whisper, "How much must I do?" It shouts, "How much can I give?"

We are free now—free to serve without fear. Free to love without calculation. Free to pour ourselves out in reckless devotion, not to be noticed, not to be praised, but because we belong to the One who gave everything for us. Because of our relationship with Jesus, we are free to serve with abandon.

Jesus taught a spectacular parable about the Prodigal Son (Luke 15.11–32). The younger son twists his father's arm for his share of the inheritance. Although the father is still alive, he gives in to the younger son. The son goes off and really lives it up. Parties. Friends. Girls. Until he goes broke. When the money runs out, the friends run off. He finds himself feeding pigs. Few things could be more disgusting or degrading for a Jewish man. And he's hungry! So hungry he contemplates eating the slop he fed the pigs. The young son goes home, he thinks, in utter disgrace. He had a speech prepared and memorized for his father. "I'm not worthy to be a son, but could you make me a servant?" He never had a chance to use the speech. His father ran to meet him. Then, the father threw a huge party in his honor. He was welcomed back as a son, even though he didn't deserve it (and even though his older brother grumbled about it.)

Let's add a sequel to Jesus' parable.

A year or two later, life has settled down to a reasonably humdrum existence again. His older brother tolerates having him around, more or less; his father is getting older. He remembers with a happy sigh the day he came up the road, and his father came running to greet him. He remembers the embrace, the robe, the ring, the feast. And he thinks, "Suppose I did it again? Why not help myself to enough things to survive, run away for a few weeks, and then play the penitent son and come back again? Could I game the system and relive the welcome? Maybe I'll get another party!"

That's not repentance. That's manipulation. And it reveals a heart that never truly came home. When you know what the Father has done for you—when you've felt the weight of sin fall off your shoulders and the warmth of His arms pull you close—you don't run away again. You run for Him. You wake up every morning wondering how to honor the One who covered your shame and called you His child.

That is the essence of piety—not a rigid system of performance, not a ladder to climb in pursuit of spiritual merit, and not a calculated strategy to manipulate divine favor. It is the wholehearted surrender of a life laid bare before God, a heart no longer driven by the need to impress others but consumed with the singular desire to bring delight to the Father.

Those who live this way will often be misunderstood. Their devotion may be questioned, their sincerity doubted, and their motives misjudged. Some will say they take things too seriously. Others will assume they are simply trying to earn attention or admiration. But the opinions of others are not the standard we live by, and their approval is not the reward we seek.

This life is not about them. It never was.

God's Smile is Enough

The ones who walk in true piety are not chasing applause, not searching for affirmation, not performing for the crowd. Their gaze is fixed on the face of God, and their deepest longing is to bring joy to His heart.

So serve with a full heart. Worship with every fiber of your being, holding nothing back. Obey the voice of the Lord with eagerness, not hesitation. Love those around you with the same grace you've been given, even when it is difficult, even when it is not returned.

He is worthy of nothing less than your all.

He is worth it.

He always has been.

He always will be.

For it is by grace you have been saved, through faith — and this not from yourselves, it is the gift of God — not by works, so that no one can boast. For we are God's workmanship, created in

Christ Jesus to do good works, which God prepared in advance for us to do.

The Road Ahead

Piety puts your hands on the wheel. The Holy Spirit fuels the engine.

You've believed. You've confessed. You've repented. You've been baptized. You've begun to live a life that reflects Jesus. But if you're honest, the road still feels uphill. You want to do good—but the good is hard. You want to say no—but the temptations are loud. You want to walk in purity—but your feet still slip.

That's not because your faith is fake. It's because your flesh is real.

No one rebuilds a car just to let it sit. You don't restore a Mustang and leave it on jack stands. You rebuilt it to run. You brought it to life so it could move. But the rebuild isn't enough without fuel. No matter how polished the paint, how strong the frame, or how perfect the restoration—without fuel, you're not going anywhere.

That's why Jesus didn't just forgive your sins. He sent His Spirit.

The Holy Spirit is not an accessory for the advanced. He is the ignition spark for every step of the journey. He is not a sidekick. He is the powertrain. Without Him, you can try harder, strive longer, push forward—but eventually, you stall. Because flesh can't drive faith. Discipline can't defeat sin. Only the Spirit can.

The life you've been called to live—pure, holy, strong, surrendered—is not sustained by passion alone. You need power. You need presence. You need fire in the tank.

Piety may be your desire. But the Holy Spirit is your fuel.

In the next book, we'll talk about that fuel.
We'll explore the power you were never meant to live without.

Because when the Spirit takes the wheel, you don't just run—you burn rubber.

www.ingramcontent.com/pod-product-compliance
Lightning Source LLC
Chambersburg PA
CBHW060427130626
46555CB00005B/2249